THE G[illegible] OF THOMAS

A SPIRITUAL INTERPRETATION FOR THE AQUARIAN AGE

THE GOSPEL OF THOMAS

A SPIRITUAL INTERPRETATION FOR THE AQUARIAN AGE

Rev. Daniel Chesbro,
with **Rev. James Erickson**

FINDHORN PRESS

Published in 2012 by Findhorn Press, Scotland

ISBN 978-1-84409-602-2

A CIP record for this title is available from the British Library.

Edited by Nicky Leach
Cover design by Sharon Ford
Interior design by Damian Keenan
Printed and bound in the USA

1 2 3 4 5 6 7 8 9 17 16 15 14 13 12

Published by
Findhorn Press
117-121 High Street,
Forres IV36 1AB,
Scotland, UK

t +44 (0)1309 690582
f +44 (0)131 777 2711
e info@findhornpress.com
www.findhornpress.com

Dedication

These inspired words, teachings, and images are presented in a fully heartfelt way to all who journey on their Spiritual path, and especially to the priests in the Order of Melchizedek. May you be enlightened by these thoughts and images to use them in your ministry of teaching and healing a world in transition in the Aquarian Age.

PREFACE

I Want to Understand

I have a habit of leaving a television set on while trying to go to sleep at night. The droning voices in a darkened room provide a "white noise" that allows me to avoid thinking, and thereby avoid reviewing my life's events—past, present, or future. Instead, I am lulled off to sleep... "perchance to dream."

Several years ago, while working for the Terra Christa bookstore in Vienna, VA, doing workshops, readings, and ordinations into the Order of Melchizedek, I was staying at a local motel, turned on the TV late one night, and went right off to sleep. When I awoke, around 3 a.m., there were film credits scrolling up the TV screen. With one eye open, I glanced at the credits for a film entitled *Stigmata,* a movie that I had not seen. Having briefly worked in motion pictures years earlier, I pay attention to the credits to see if I might recognize someone's name. A credit rolled by for "The Gospel of Thomas." The Gospel of Thomas? Having been in three seminaries, I know the gospels of Matthew, Mark, Luke, and John—Thomas I don't know.

I rolled over, pulled up the blanket, and went back to sleep, leaving the TV volume on low so that I could hardly hear it, but loud enough to keep me from "thinking."

In the morning I showered, shaved, dressed, and went to breakfast. It was a short drive to the bookstore and to work. As I opened the door to Terra Christa, I was confronted by a full display of the book, *The Gospel of Thomas*! I smiled. Obviously, the Universe had put the book in my path. I bought a copy and couldn't wait to see what this gospel entailed and where it came from.

Later that day, during a work break, I began to glance through the 114 sayings attributed to the Master Jesus by a follower named Judas. This is not the Judas Iscariot found in the bible, but another man also named Judas who was a twin and follower of The Master Jesus. This gospel would therefore have to be an earlier work than the three gospels of Matthew, Luke, and John, and perhaps truer to the original teachings of Jesus. Exhilarated now to read further, I was dismayed when I was not able to understand these profound parables. My mind could not grasp the scope of these sayings, and I put the book aside.

Weeks later, while leaving to go on another business trip, I retrieved the Book of Thomas and took it to read on the plane. After fastening my seat belt and putting my tray table in an upright and locked position, I anxiously waited for the plane to take off so that I could get my book from my carryon and begin to read (and hopefully understand this time). I got the book and started to read the first parable, but still could not get my head into it. Frustrated, I took a breath and said a thought-filled prayer: "God, please, I want to understand. I desire to know."

Now at 30,000 feet and climbing, my mind opened like a steel door and I grabbed a pen and paper and started to take notes as if taking dictation. *Number One*, it began . . . and I had to write as fast as I could to keep up. Over the next few days, the dictation continued until I had completed all 114 sayings.

"Now what?" I asked myself.

The answer came instantly: *You are to teach these sayings. These sayings are important to the spiritual understanding of God's unconditional love and compassion.*

A month or so later, I offered the sayings to a small group in a workshop. However, their reaction seemed less than enthusiastic, so I came home and, once again, put the sayings aside.

After my book, *The Order of Melchizedek: Love, Willing Service, and Fulfillment* (Findhorn, 2010), was completed, and my next book, *Tom Sawyer: Messenger from God,* was in the editing phase, Spirit said, *Now go get the Thomas material. That is the next manuscript*. So with trepidation and not knowing if I would understand what had already been so freely provided, I sat down to work, breathed and focused, and again the dictation began (*Number One*...). In a few days, all 114 sayings had been expanded and fully completed.

I drew the illustrations that appear with the sayings myself, but the most difficult part of the endeavor was typing all of the materials to send to my friend and co-writer/editor, Jim Erickson, for his final touches. I asked Jim to read the original texts found in the Nag Hammadi and to read my interpretation, then, as with *The Order of Melchizedek: Love, Willing Service, and Fulfillment*, to edit, add, subtract, wordsmith the material, and so on. The book you hold in your hands was not put together with that volume in mind, but the two dovetail and complement each other quite nicely.

This is not an academic endeavor; it is meant to be inspirational and uplifting. The translations may not be entirely accurate, but they capture the essence of the meaning of the sayings of Jesus. This work may be read and used in many ways.

For example, you can read it straight through, use it as a daily meditation guide, or simply hold an intention and open it randomly to a saying when you want inspiration or help.

What follows is the result of the inspirational dictations that were given me for *The Gospel of Thomas: An Inspirational Interpretation for the Aquarian Age*.

INTRODUCTION

How It All Began & What It's All About

The Gospel of Thomas does not tell a story nor is it a narration of the life of Jesus. Instead, it is a collection of sayings, prophecies, proverbs, and parables of Jesus. Some of these are familiar, as we know them from Matthew and Luke: Jesus said, "I have come to cast fire on the earth." Or "Behold, a sower went out to sow. . . ," and so forth. Others are as strange and compelling as Zen koans.

What is typical about these sayings is that they claim that if you want to understand what Jesus said, you have to recognize yourself—you have to know yourself. Furthermore, it is noteworthy that this work claims that the proper understanding of these sayings themselves leads to life eternal. For example: "Whosoever discovers the interpretation of these sayings will not taste death" (Saying 1).

The Coptic Gospel of Thomas was translated from the Greek, and fragments of this Greek version have been preserved. It dates to about A.D. 200 (C.E.) and is thought to have been written in Syria, Palestine, or Mesopotamia. Thus, the Greek (or even Aramaic) collection was composed in the period before about A.D. 200 (C.E.), and maybe as early as the second half of the first century.

As I mentioned, the authorship of the Gospel of Thomas is attributed to Didymos Judas Thomas, Judas "the Twin," an apostle of Jesus. The name Thomas in Aramaic (*Tau'ma*) means "twin," while Didymos is Greek for twin, also. Matthew (10:1–3) named Didymos Judas Thomas an apostle, as did Mark (3:14–18) and Luke (6:13–15). The Syrian Christians believed Didymos Judas Thomas was the twin brother of Jesus. In the Book of Thomas the Contender, a text detailing the dialogue between the risen Jesus and Judas Thomas before the ascension of Jesus, Jesus refers to him as "brother," "twin," and "friend." However, that Didymos Judas Thomas might be the fraternal twin of Jesus seems problematic, at least from an orthodox theological point of view, for there is no mention anywhere in the New Testament that Mary had twins. It could be that Didymos Judas Thomas was a member of the inner circle of Jesus and had been given deeper teachings, and/or had become a highly evolved Spiritual being that led to him being called metaphorically the "twin" of Jesus.

The Coptic text of the Gospel of Thomas was supposedly discovered with the Nag Hammadi library in December 1945, and this gospel is the second tractate (document) of Codex II. The story of the discovery was told by an Egyptian, Muhammad Ali, a member of the al-Samman clan. Apparently, he and several *fellahin* were riding their camels near the Jabal al-Tarif, a cliff along the Nile River not far from the current city of Nag Hammadi. They were in search of a natural fertilizer, *sabakh*, that could be found in that area. Dismounted and on foot, they came to the face of the cliff, which was strewn with debris, and began to dig around a boulder.

What they found was a large storage jar with a bowl sealed to the top as a lid. They were slow to open this jar, apprehensive that it might contain a *jinn* (spirit), which, if released, could haunt them or do other misdeeds. Yet they were also aware of the legends of treasures hidden in the region. Apparently they weighed the pro and cons, and their desire for gold overcame their fear of jinns, and they smashed the jar. According to Muhammad Ali, a golden substance flew out of the jar and dispersed in the air.

Was this a jinn? Perhaps, but it's not likely. It is believed that what he saw was exceedingly fine particles of the papyrus, gold in color from age, which glinted in the sunlight. Inside the jar were thirteen papyrus books, or codices, of the Nag Hammadi library—the Gospel of Thomas was part of this library.

The Gospel of Thomas was probably one of the earliest texts (other than the canonical gospels) to offer the teachings of Jesus, but it was not included in the New Testament canon, perhaps because the "canonizers" considered it to contain heresy. Then again, it may have been sidelined because it lacked any mention of the death and resurrection of Jesus—information the four chosen gospels include. However, the Epistles and the Book of Revelation do not mention stories of the demise of Jesus, and they are included.

Simply put, the whys and wherefores that led to the exclusion of the Gospel of Thomas remain points of debate among biblical scholars. Some historians feel that the Gospel of Thomas should not be labeled a Gnostic text. The Gnostics loved their mythology, but the Gospel of Thomas contains no myths. Still, some parts of the manuscript appear to have a Gnostic bent, and therefore there is disagreement on this point, too. If versions of Gnostic thought existed in pre-Christian Judaism, it is possible that Thomas, a Jew, may have been aware of it. It is also conceivable that some of the more Gnostic of the sayings were added to the gospel. So again, whether the Gospel of Thomas is or is not a Gnostic text is another point of debate among biblical scholars.

The synoptic gospels depict Jesus as a unique being. The Gospel of John says that Jesus isn't even a human being at all but a divine presence who comes down from Heaven in human shape: "God sent his son into the world to save the world." If you believe in him, you're saved; if you don't believe in him, you're already damned because you haven't believed in the name of the only begotten Son of God.

The Jesus in the Gospel of Thomas appears to be somewhat different from the Jesus of the synoptic gospels. What you discover as you read the Gospel of Thomas—which you're meant to discover—is that, at a deep level, it is YOU and Jesus who are identical twins. You discover that you are the child of God, just as Jesus is. In the Gospel of Thomas the disciples say to Jesus: "Tell us. What do you want us to do? How shall we pray? What shall we eat? How shall we fast?" In the Gospel of Thomas, Jesus does not answer these questions. He simply says: "Do not tell lies, and do not do what you hate, for everything is known before Heaven."

This answer throws you and me upon ourselves. In this gospel, in effect, Jesus turns one toward oneself. That is really one of the themes of the Gospel of Thomas—that you must go on a sort of spiritual quest of your own to discover who you are, and to discover that you really are the child of God, just like Jesus. Indeed, at the end of this gospel, Jesus speaks to Thomas and says: "Whoever drinks from my mouth will become as I am, and I will become that person, and the mysteries will be revealed to him."

Punctuation Guide

In some of the sayings you will find unfamiliar punctuation marks. These are the meanings:

- Bold brackets around ellipses (**[...]**) means that there is text missing from the original—that we do not know what word or words were there.

- A saying ending with ellipses and closing quotation marks (**...“**) indicates that we do not know the final words.

- Sentences separated with elipses (**xxxxx.” ... “xxxxx**) indicate missing words.

- Parentheses enclosing content **(xxxxx.)** are the editor’s words added to clarify meaning.

1

"He or she who comprehends the interpretation of these sayings will never taste death."

Energy cannot be destroyed; rather, it mutates or evolves—creation and evolution! There is no part of the universe, visible or invisible, that experiences death, only eternal life and light. That light is unconditional love, which is the body of the universe and an expression and function of the Light of God.

Everyone in the physical body will experience dying physically. Since the time of Melchizedek, when sexual union became the sole means by which the human condition would propagate the human race, death of the physical was assured. Understand, however, that physical death is merely another form of evolution.

Melchizedek had a fourth-dimensional body, and as an avatar was "down to earth" in enough physical mass and form to be present. However, the "body" of Melchizedek was not born of woman but out of the "mind" of God and, as such, never experienced a physical body death. He was never born of woman and he never died physically but left the earth plane through spontaneous combustion. From the time of Melchizedek on, whenever God came into any incarnation or intended to come into the earth plane, He/She experienced physical body birth and physical death.

These teachings and never dying refer to the elimination of ignorance and fear and to the attainment of enlightenment, which is the awareness of eternal Life and Light to human consciousness—a lifting of the veil, so to speak. Once one is enlightened, that full attainment of consciousness never diminishes, passes away, nor dies. Instead, old thought forms pass away as new evident Truths come into our awareness. "I was a child and perceived as a child, but now I am an adult and all of the childish ways are put behind me . . . "

In ancient Egypt, there was a myth about the death of the goddess Isis. After Isis died, she was buried near Memphis and a statue was erected to her, covered from head to toe with a black veil. It was written of her, "I am all that has been, that is, and that shall be and none among mortals has yet dared to raise my veil." "Anyone who lifts this veil will surely die!"

Moses was brought up as an Egyptian prince and was schooled in all the ancient mysteries, including the myths of Isis. After Moses encountered God on Mount Zion, it was written that he wore a veil (Ex 34:30) and only took it off when he and Joshua talked to God (Joshua was a later reincarnation of Melchizedek). Moses wore a veil over his face so that his people would not come to know the full brilliance of his enlightenment—so they would neither fear him nor God.

There was also a veil in the Holy Temple in Jerusalem, separating the Holy of Holies from the rest of the inner temple. Only after much preparation was the High Priest permitted to pass through the veil and enter into the Holy of Holies, where he would commune with God. When Jesus (a later incarnation of Melchizedek) was crucified, a storm rose up, an earthquake occurred, and the temple veil was severed, leaving the Holy of Holies open and accessible.

The outer courtyard of the temple symbolized the outer consciousness and physical world—the Conscious Mind. The inner temple symbolized the Unconscious Mind, and the Holy of Holies represented the Super Conscious Mind. Lifting the veil, or bissecting it (symbolizing the comprehension of these teachings and the elimination of ignorance and fear), allows for greater access to God, and there is only God and there is only Good.

Conceptually, "death" is a form of ignorance—to be asleep in one's life and blind to Truth. In the fourth dimension there is only Truth, not relative Truth but Universal Truth. With the lack of knowledge of Universal Truth in the third dimension, it is as if we are sleep walking, existing without the assuredness of knowing, and thus without the elimination of fear. But a person coming to comprehend these sayings and teachings will realize that life and love are eternal; that the process of physical body death is an expectation of the life beyond, and there will be no dying with fear. As you learn to accept and love yourself unconditionally—as God loves you—you can move naturally into Grace—the bliss of being One with God. There are no veils of separation from beliefs in pure consciousness.

Paramahansa Yogananda, knowing of his impending physical body death, held a dinner party. After the dinner, he slumped in his seat and passed, but he never decomposed. You, too, can become aware of your time of passing or death, usually previewed in your dreamtime and with intuition, and simply step out of your body when your work here is done. Simply go back in memory to that place within you where the knowledge and memory of being one with God resides, and step into the Light. Life is eternal, and the Light is eternal. The universe does not die but reincarnates forever in love, harmony, and balance. Lift the veils of ignorance from your mind, release all fears, and know eternal life.

Since the time that God imagined you and gave you a soul with free will, you have possessed the gift of eternal life. Through many incarnations, you have grown and evolved to achieve the state of being one with God in eternal and unconditional love—no separation, no ignorance, no veil. Only freedom! He or she who comprehends the interpretation of these sayings will never taste death.

2

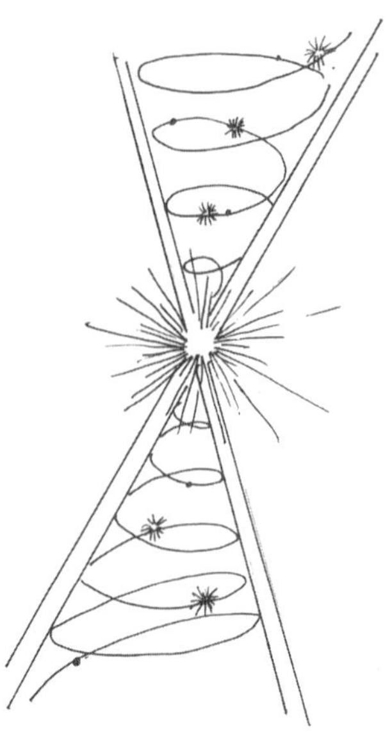

"Let him who seeks continue seeking until he finds. And when he finds he will become troubled. When he becomes troubled he will be astonished, and he will rule over all."

To seek is to be able to find. This is the Law of Karma—balanced cause and effect in action. Once you find what you have been seeking, new questions and levels of awareness may arise. New thresholds to cross with more growth, spirituality, and events of enlightenment may occur. God is the past, the present, and the future simultaneously, and yet in God there is no time. So too, total knowledge has no end but is ongoing in the unfolding of the universe.

When, in the present, you pursue your probable futures and find them in the mind of God, you have reached Akasha. This will open up and reveal many ways of understanding. Knowing or having access beyond fear of all probable futures can give you the sense of "ruling over all" in your choice of future probable events through the use of your free will. And, comprehending what you may have learned from the past (even past lives), accepting the present as an expression of the result of all past life choices, and "seeing into the future" by dreams, precognitions, and intuitions, you are free to take conscious responsibility in this lifetime—free to rule over all.

The knowledge of present life and transforming all thoughts of it through unconditional love, which is not judgment but loving acceptance, gives you freedom, expands your mind, and uplifts your heart.

"Be ye not troubled nor confused because I am with you!"

3

"If those who lead you say, 'See, the Kingdom is in the sky,' then the birds of the sky will precede you. If they say, 'It is in the sea,' then the fish will precede you. Rather, the Kingdom is inside you, and it is also outside you. When you come to know yourself, then you will become known, and you will realize that it is you who are the sons of the living Father. But if you will not know yourselves you will dwell in poverty, and it is you who are that poverty."

The birds in the air are not seeking consciousness; they are the creation and evolution of God's unconditional love. They do not possess free will but are the will of God continuously expressing itself. They are God becoming, and have no sense of "separation" from God, whereas we may create the space of separation in choosing not to believe in God and in God's unconditional love. We are free to create "hell on earth" through doubting and being skeptical, and we are free to end that separation by simply loving ourselves.

The Kingdom of God is an eternal idea; it has no ending. It is God's body in the universe, both visible and invisible. Know yourself in all ways possible—through dreams, astrology, numerology, palmistry, and so on—for the path from the past in the present may reveal the future probabilities that you co-created with God before the beginning of any time.

God is expressing all life and all life forms, both visible and invisible. However, the birds and the fish will not have nor need a life review, nor experience self-judgment in karma. Only the souls of free will will have that experience.

When you know yourself fully in consciousness, you may also be recognized by others as such, and you will know that you are, as well as all things, one with God. But if you fail to know yourself and instead dwell in a house of ignorance, with thought forms of fear and lack, then you will always be "poor" in Spirit and in Truth. God will not violate your free will, and so if you see yourself as poor and/or a victim, you will remain in those thoughts until you change your mind. Love yourself as God does and be free, and then you will live in a different state of being—in the Kingdom of God.

When you pass over from this life you will go to a place called Paradise, and the lights in Paradise are called Heaven. The birds are already aware of this, as are the fish of the sea, as they live in the mind of God as an eternal thought. You do also, but if you do not love yourself, and if you choose to live in the imagination of separation, God cannot enter into your thought forms because of your free will. Free will and God are equal in power. This is God's supreme gift of unceasing love to you.

"An old man will not hesitate to ask a small child seven days old about the place of life, and he will live. For many who are first will become last, and they will become one and the same."

Wise in years, you may ask a person circumcised or not for Truth and receive it. All are acceptable to God; there are no conditions. All possess Truth since all are from the One, and a child young in years may retain his or her innocence and not be polluted by society and culture. ("Out of the mouths of babes.")

Using reincarnation and karma from your first created lifetime, when you achieved a soul and free will, you have utilized your choices and mind to create that life, the one you now live and the ones to come. For as Buddha said: "What you are is what you have been, what you do now is what you will be." So you are the results of all of your past lives from the beginning, and this life is the singular result of all of the others, whatever dimension or plane of existence you have expressed yourself into. The first becomes the last, and the last is the expression of the first life. The union of all of your past lives is the single life that you are now living.

To amend karma, change your thoughts about yourself or selves in your past in the present and thereby change the future of probable lives. Love cancels karma, even 10,000 years of karma, so forgive, release, and let go.

You may wish to return to this plane, or another, to continue to learn about love and to teach and to heal. Some do this by taking the vow of the Bodhisatva: "I will incarnate until the last being wakes up." Whatever you decide, choose life and celebrate.

5

"Recognize what is in your sight, and that which is hidden will become plain to you. There is nothing hidden which will not become manifest."

Come to know all of who and what you are, and what is not known to you can then be revealed. ("Know thyself!") That which appears to be hidden is knowable by looking at your perfect past(s) or knowing your probable future(s). In this way, nothing can be hidden or not known by you.

A life review, whether as the result of a near-death experience or through spontaneous awakening, can remove all self-doubts and fears, as you are the result of all of your thoughts and actions, and God will love you unconditionally, who knows all and is all. Everything comes into your life review, which happens with each death. All of the events, from conception to the day you die, all dreams, all knowledge of attending events, will be revealed and revealed without God's judgment. Remember: God is an unconditional lover: God will only love you. You will judge yourself in your life review: What did you choose to do with the life you were given? What did you choose to learn? And what did you choose to love? You are the result of all your thoughts and choices. So possess self-acceptance and unconditional self-love, as God already has for you. This frees you up in the present and prepares you for your future in this life and future lives.

You have the power to forgive, release, and let go of any pasts, in the present, and for all futures.

6

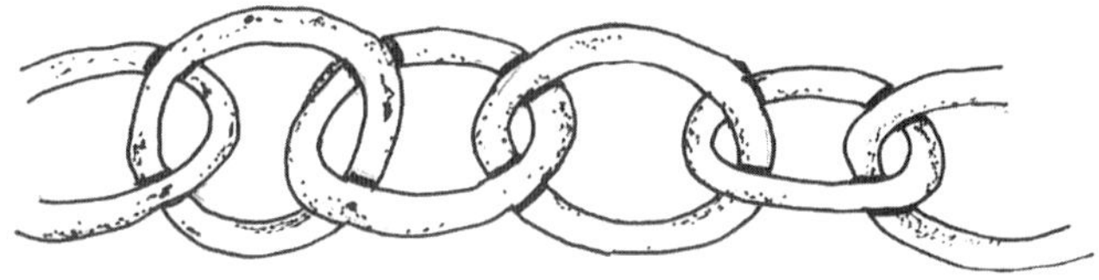

"Don't tell lies and do not do what you hate, for all things are plain in the sight of Heaven. Nothing hidden will not become manifest, and nothing covered will remain without being uncovered."

Live in harmony with all parts of the laws. Avoid creating pollutions either in your mind or out of your mouth with words, for words have power. Therefore, do not bear false witness and do not hate in thought or deed, for only you will live in your hatreds and not the person or situation that you created and held hatred for.

Likewise, prayer can be thoughts, words, and/or feelings created by you, and all are acceptable to God. So live your life as if it were always in prayer and talking to God. Pray over your food before you eat it and after you eat it, so that it is blessed to all parts of you.

Do not go against your own free will. For example, if you dislike to fast, then don't do it.

Honor those who have created poverty[1] on all levels. If they choose to be free, then they can be free, but judge not, for you have no idea what they are choosing to learn nor what their karma holds.

To give to charity is to receive in charity. If you are a great giver, then you must also be a great receiver, for that is the law. By allowing others to give to you, with your permission, you are allowing love and energy to return to you, and this is how God replenishes.

Whatsoever you choose to do will be disclosed by you and for you. You will understand in your life review just what your thoughts and actions lead to in behavior and creation, and then what that led to in the lives of those impacted. Then all will be disclosed to you, for already all is known by God, who loves you unconditionally, eternally, and without judgment.

1 When you truly come to know yourself you'll understand your divinity, and also understand your mortality. In this way you'll recognize that mortality is really meaningless, as physical existence is meaningless. Therefore, death is no longer a problem but a solution, because in death all this mortality will fall away, and the true self will be liberated to an independent existence no longer dependent on the physical, nor on what goes with physical existence, such as sickness, poverty, and so on. This is why physical existence is often described as poverty. Thus, when you truly know yourself you are no longer in poverty.

7

"Blessed is the lion, which becomes man when devoured by man; and cursed is the man whom the lion devours, and the lion becomes man."

When you consume foods, whether animal or vegetable, that which you eat becomes you and enables you to continue in your present form. All is energy and consumes energy to continue, and there is no death. The exchange of energies is necessary for life to continue. Water, food, and sex are the main drives of the human condition, and you need all three to be balanced. If you are consumed by some beast, your life force goes to give that beast added life.

The human condition is both animal and spiritual. Lower nature (from our point of view) is animal, and the higher nature is spiritual, and in the human condition possesses the gift of free will. Animals are encased in a flesh body and have no free will. Fish, fowl, plant kingdoms, animals, and so forth are the will of God expressing itself through creation and evolution. But all are life and divine in nature, for there is only God and there is only Good.

8

"The man is like a wise fisherman who cast his net into the sea and drew it up full of small fish. Among them the fisherman found a fine large fish. He threw all the small fish back and chose the large fish without difficulty. Whoever has ears to hear, let him hear."

As you live, throw back the "little things in life" and hold fast to the greater. All are good, but weigh the justice of all. Avoid holding onto the things and situations in life that are less significant, or in time they will prove to be so. This is to say, forgive, release, and let go. Be as a man or woman who fishes and release the small ones and takes the prize catch to eat and feed others, even the thousands. So discard the petty stuff, for if you dwell on it you will build a petty prison for yourself and lock yourself inside. Let go and let God!

9

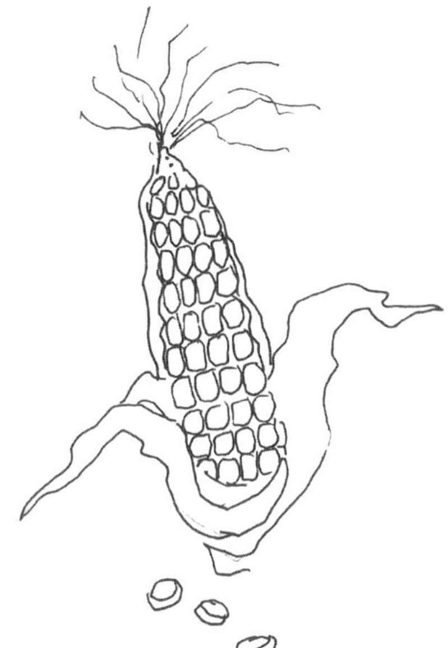

"The sower went out taking a handful of seeds and scattered them. Some fell on the road, where the birds came and gathered them up. Others fell on rock, where they did not take root in the soil and did not produce ears. Others fell on thorns; they choked the seeds and worms ate them. But others fell on the good soil, and it produced good fruit: it bore sixty per measure and a hundred and twenty per measure."

The parable of sowing the good seeds refers to thought forms cast out from your head and mind. All thoughts have the ability to become things and deeds. If you "sow" with good intent and cast out seed thoughts they will take root and provide a great abundance. One kernel of corn, placed in the right environment, can yield many ears of corn, and so too thoughts and deeds. Understand that it is your intention that is the "rain" that produces a crop of abundance, or lack thereof. Words have power, and emotions coupled with words have even more power in creativity and creation. Choose your words, emotions, thoughts, and intentions with care.

10

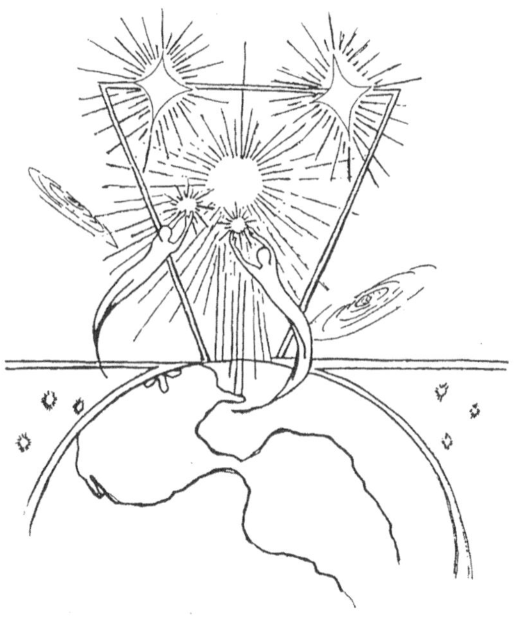

"I have cast fire upon the world, and look,
I am guarding it until it blazes."

I have brought consciousness and enlightenment into the world. Messengers of Truth have come into the human condition, and some with spontaneous awakening or near death awakening are now working in the field. In time their labors will produce a giant light, as if the world were on fire. Fire transforms and changes the old ways of being and thinking and makes the new possible. The old ways were destroyed by water and a flood. The new world will be cleansed by the fires of consciousness and Truth—at first just a flame, and then an intense conflagration. The old things pass away, and behold, I make all things new. The world is to be filled with enlightenment and equality.

11

"This Heaven will pass away, and the one above it will pass away. The dead are not alive, and the living will not die. In the days when you devoured what is dead, you made it what is alive. When you come to dwell in the light, what will you do? On the day when you were one you became two. And when you become two, what will you do?"

It takes billions of years for the universe to expand and only millions of years for it to contract: the Big Bang followed by the Big Crunch—the Universe breathing in and out. This is the fourth time that time will come to an end. When this era passes away, a new one will be born and will not be a carbon-based unit, which is the matrix that you are now. In the third dimension, you eat other species and plants in order to stay in the physical form. Beyond this time, there will be other means by which you will sustain life. So, too, future times may require other means for a soul's expression, but there is no death, and you will never die nor cease to exist.

Those who are not awake spiritually are as those asleep or dead. Whether they choose to be enlightened or not, let them be. For they remain in perfection for as long and in as many lifetimes as they so choose. Judge them not, for it is none of your concern. Let the dead bury their own dead. You may pray for them that one day they will not be blind (or dead) to their divine natures, and that they, too, will have ears to hear.

When you came into form you began as one, both yin and yang. But as you came into human form, you split and chose a predominant force of yin or yang, and possessed a soul that is in balance to both. You are here to learn about love and creativity, and by being in a split form of yin or yang you learn to possess life experience. Therefore, woman, love your male side, and man, love your female side, for bringing them together in love is what Oneness is all about. When you make your transition, you will experience being in and of the Light, and possess the freedom to experience creativity with different constraints, or not.

12

"Wherever you are, go to James the Righteous, for whose sake Heaven and Earth came into being."[2]

Who are your leaders in this new age of Aquarius? In the future, only those who are truly spiritual shall be elected or appointed to positions of leadership. Therefore, follow the path of righteousness and live in egalitarianism for all sentient beings. Unconditional self-love, and the love for others in all dimensions and expressions, is necessary.

2 aka James the Lesser (Jacobus Minor), James the Younger, James the Small, or James the Just. Infrequently referred to as James the Supplanter (in probable reference to Jesus). The cousin of Jesus (son of Mary, the sister of Marium the mother of Jesus), brother of Jude Thaddeus. One of the first to have visions of the risen Christ. First bishop of Jerusalem, serving in this position for thirty years. He is reported to have spent so much time on his knees in prayer for the people that his knees thickened and looked like a camel's knees. He lived an ascetic lifestyle—supposedly he drank neither wine nor strong drink, ate no flesh, never shaved or anointed himself with ointment, or bathed. He was held in such high esteem and viewed as so righteous that he is said to have had the privilege of entering the Holy of Holies in the Temple. Saying No. 12 implies that we are to choose "James-like" individuals for our counsel and to be our leaders.

13

"I am not your master. Because you have drunk, you have become intoxicated from the spring which I have measured out."

They drank from the well of Wisdom, Knowledge, and Truth and became "drunk." If higher truths are given you, be careful how you present them to those who would listen and follow you. ("Don't feed babies meat but milk.") You will be judged by your actions, and not just the words that come out of your mouth. Balance your wisdom with humor and creativity, and be the example for others. You are your own teachers.

14

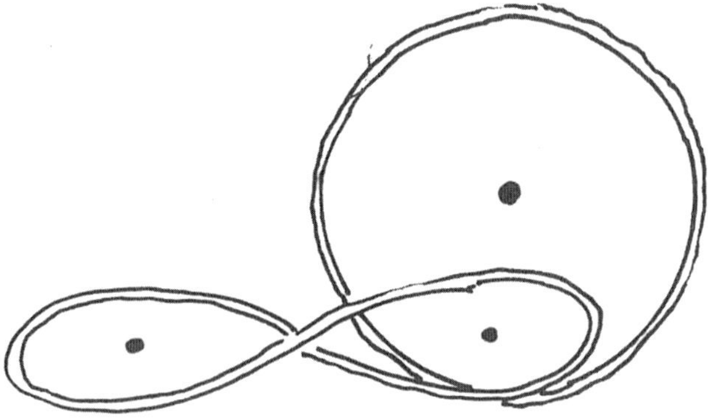

"If you fast, you will give rise to sin for yourselves. If you pray, you will be condemned. If you give alms, you will do harm to your spirit. So when you go into any land, if they receive you, eat what they will set before you, and heal the sick among them. For what goes into your mouth will not defile you, but that which issues from your mouth—that's what will defile you."

In prayer, what are you asking? Pray and let go of the prayer, so that the Universe can bring it to you. Pray with love and gratitude, for what is and for what you are intending. Pray as if it were already yours, for to do otherwise is casting thoughts into the tide of the ocean, and that will take the result away from you. Then, too, in giving to charity, if your intention is not clear, the result will come back to haunt you. Instead, give freely and lovingly, and be prepared to receive in the same manner and in the same spirit, for all is cause and effect and energies magnify as they are called into being: that which you send out come back multiplied.

Whatsoever you eat or drink, be grateful and give thanks. God is all, and all that you take and consume. To think otherwise brings with the consumed energies a taint of fear, so the savor will be bitter to your taste.

Heal the sick with their consent. If they allow you to heal them but you have not asked, it will not last. Know that free will prevails, so ask: "May I offer you a healing energy?" This constitutes both an invitation to the Spirit and acknowledges free will. Then the two or more are gathered together and the magic takes place. ("I am with you.")

What goes into your mouth is made of God, as all things are. But what you may create by what comes out of your mouth in your speech, if ill intended, can defile you. The energy returns to the creator, magnified, and does the bidding of its master. All is in your intention, because without right intent the end thought form will be adversity. If you start with joy in your heart, then the whole experience will lighten the spirit.

15

"When you see one who was not born of a woman, prostrate yourselves on your faces and worship him, for that one is your Father."

Honor that which is of God. Worship, love, and adore it, for it is the innocence of creation. Amelius, Adam, Hermes, Enoch, and Melchizedek were not born of woman but out of the word of God made manifest. They were not born of woman and did not experience physical body death, but left the earth plane through spontaneous combustion; they desired to become one again with God, and so it was done.

After Melchizedek, all of the intrusions into the human condition were born of woman and died a physical body death, even Jesus the Christ.

16

"Men think that it is peace which I have come to cast upon the world.
They do not know that it is dissension which I have come to cast:
fire, sword, and war. For there will be five in the house:
three will be against two, and two against three;
the Father against the son and the son against the Father.
And they will stand alone."

Change comes with new thought forms. New ideas challenge the old and result in discord. If you are to stand alone, hold onto the Truth, and be steadfast in your witness. In time, Truth prevails and will win out over all, even to the end of the age.

17

"I will give you what no eye has seen and what no ear has heard and what no hand has touched and what has never occurred to the human mind."

If there be only a spark of light, then there can be no darkness. A distant flicker of light now becomes bright and a flame. When I tell you that there is only one God and only Good, your higher self knows this to be true and remembers it. The new thought is of a God who is your eternal and unconditional lover. The peace I give you the world cannot give, and has not known.

18

"Have you discovered that at the beginning you look for the end?
Where the beginning is, there the end will be also.
Blessed is he who will take his place in the beginning,
for he will know the end and will not experience death."

There is no end but only one continuous creation—a living, expanding, and contracting love—Alpha and Omega, then Alpha again. I Am that I Am is a constant from which all of creation comes into being and evolves forever, always perfect, balanced, and harmonious—in no time and in no space, only love. When you are awake you know there is only life, so then when your physical body dies you will not be in fear, and go into the Light. Awakened and enlightened consciousness knows no fear of death. It knows that death results in life, and life results in death, and death is an illusion.

19

"Blessed is he who came into being before he came into being. When you become my disciples and listen to my words, the stones will minister to you. There are five trees for you in Paradise, which remain undisturbed summer and winter and whose leaves do not fall. Whoever becomes acquainted with them will not experience death."

Before the world was I Am. Jesus was born enlightened and brought that awareness into the world. Buddha became enlightened by desire and brought that light into the world.

A mountain is made of pebbles and stones. Even stones are of God and consciousness, but a mountain can be a collection of doubts, skepticisms, and/or ignorance. If I say to the mountains move, then they will move, for a stone once asked a young man:"Would you like to move a mountain? It is very simple, all you need is patience and a teaspoon." So, too, you can move a mountain of doubts and fears by changing your mind—changing your attitude and belief. A change in attitude or belief can shift a galaxy. In this way, the stones minister to you.

The five trees in Paradise of God and consciousness are the five centers in the Tree of Life from the kabbala: Earth, Water, Fire, Air, and Spirit. These are the same elements and energies of the Great Pyramid in Giza, Egypt ("pyramid" means the fire in the middle, or middle pillar). The Middle Pillar from the Tree of Life and the kabbala is the teaching of Melchizedek, and a method of meditation for healing and for achieving enlightenment—of setting yourself afire. ("If you eat of the fruit of this tree, ye shall be like gods.") These five centers reside within you—in your temple. Your heart is the door to your temple, and your mind is the Holy of Holies, where you meet God by day and by night. If you know these things and are aware of them in your consciousness, then you are not blind, not ignorant, and not asleep—but forever alive.

20

"It [the Kingdom of Heaven] is like a mustard seed,
which is the smallest of all seeds.
But when it falls on tilled soil it produces a great plant
and becomes a shelter for the birds of the sky."

Love unlocked, chosen freely with free will, is like prepared good soil for seed, and seed thoughts can thrive and produce a great abundance of food and comfort for all. Be a sower of good seeds, tend the garden, water the ground, and then comes the abundant harvest, for I am with you always.

The garden is the world and all the beings in and of the earth—all sentient beings. Weed the garden, removing negative energies using forgiveness and justice. Water with passion and compassion. The harvest is those who have awakened and are enlightened, full of Truth and Light.

21

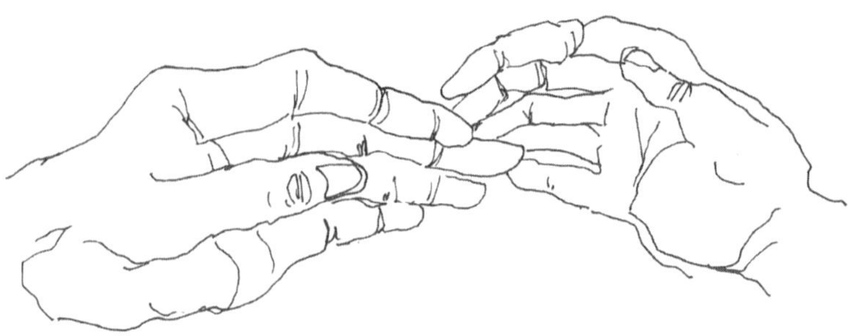

"They (my disciples) are like children who have settled in a field which is not theirs. When the owners of the field come, they'll say, 'Let us have our field back.' They (my disciples) will undress in their presence in order to let them have their field back, and to give it back to them. If the owner of a house knows that the thief is coming, he will begin his vigil and will not let him into his domain to carry away his goods. So be on your guard against the world. Arm yourselves with great strength lest the robbers find a way to come to you, for the difficulty that you expect will surely materialize. Let there be among you a person of understanding. When the grain ripened, he came quickly with his sickle and reaped it. Whoever has ears to hear, let him hear."

My followers are ignorant and innocent in their ignorance. They are like little children: they don't know what powers they possess—what is theirs by divine gift—and they may unwittingly give it all up. Don't give away your power. Your power is your free will, which is equal to the power of God. It is your ability to create out of pure thought and love, which you also possess. After all, you are made in the image and likeness of God.

If you worry about and expect troubles, then you have just fed your fears by granting them energies, and day by day they will grow and come to sit on your head. Whatever you fear will find you. This is the Law of Cause and Effect.

Take what is yours, and be willing to receive as well as give, for if you will not receive you will not be able to give.

Your harvest is God.

22

"When you make the two one; when you make the inside like the outside and the outside like the inside and the above like the below; and when you make the male and female one and the same, so that the male isn't male nor the female female; and when you make eyes in place of an eye, and a hand in place of a hand, and a foot in place of a foot, and a likeness in place of a likeness; then will you enter the Kingdom."

When you know Oneness and that you are One, and possess it, though you be split, male or female, yin or yang, you are still One. There is no separation in height nor depth, nor gender, nor in mind, unless you choose it to be so. So know Oneness and live it. Then knowing Oneness, learn to create out of it, and all comes to you and through you. ("Whatsoever you shall ask, shall be granted to you.") There is only God and there is only Good. There is only the One, and the many are of the One from the beginning.

23

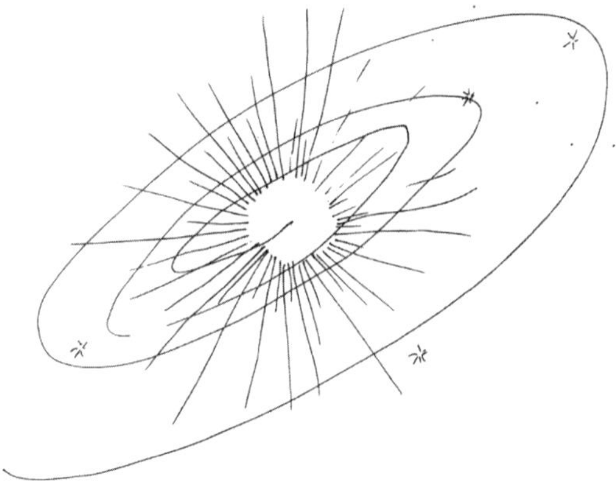

"I shall choose you, one out of a thousand, and two out of ten thousand, and these shall stand as a single one."

Be like a monk or nun who answers "the call" and be one of a kind. Start as a single one in Oneness, being witness to the One, and stand in the Truth.

24

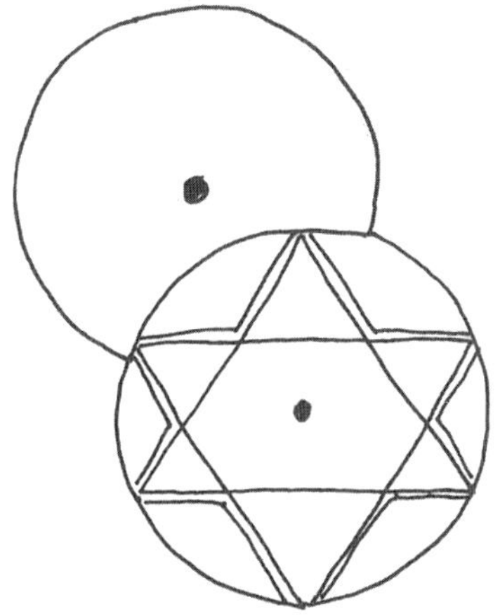

*"Whosoever has ears, let him hear.
There is light within a man of light, and he lights up the whole world.
But if he does not shine he is darkness."*

Light is the source of the heart, and the heart is the door to the temple. A spark of the divine resides in the center of the heart and remembers whence it came and where it will go. Ignorance or lack of knowing is the darkness, while freedom comes from the spark of that light in the heart. Darkness is self-perceived separation from God and from Love. But this is only a thought form of personal ignorance and cannot be the Truth, for God is the spark of Light and Truth within you, and therefore, ultimately there is no darkness.

25

"Love your brother like your soul and guard him like the pupil of your eye."

We are all a function of light from the Creator, so maintain unconditional love for all sentient beings. In Truth there is only One, and loving One is loving all. Your brothers and sisters are also the stone people, tree people, the winged ones, the four-legged, and everything that crawls or creeps upon the earth and resides in Paradise. Therefore, open your eyes and see all things with insight and love. Love God with all of your mind, heart, and soul and your neighbor as yourself.

26

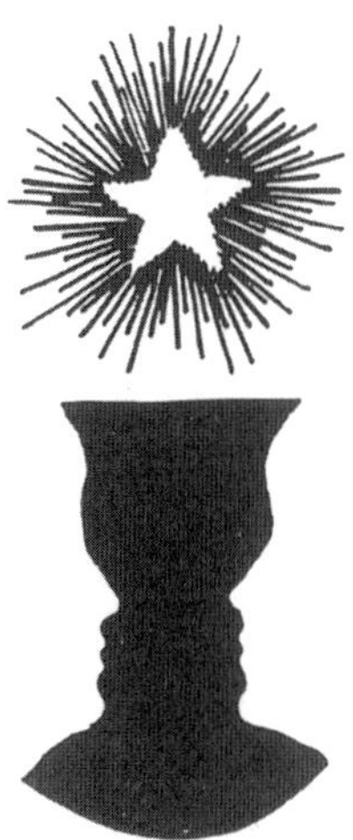

"You see the mote in your brother's eye, but not the beam in your own eye. When you cast the beam out of your own eye, then you will see clearly to cast the mote out of your brother's eye."

See yourself clearly and know yourself clearly in the light of unconditional love, and equally hold and see others in that light, for what you perceive in others is a reflection of your own ego and self. Know it and recognize it as a part of your own nature, then love it and offer help to your neighbor in opening his or her eyes.

27

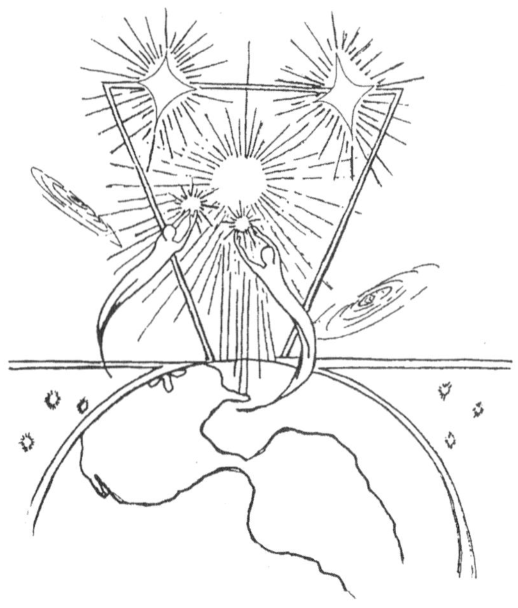

"If you do not fast from the world, you will not find the Kingdom.
If you do not observe the sabbath as a sabbath,
you will not see the Father."

Know the substance of creation—even of the world. Know the world and be detached from it at the same time. ("Be in the world but not of the world.") Detachment leads to understanding beyond illusions and results in true objectivity. The world is a part of God's body, from the least to the greatest. It is a schoolroom and a place for you, as co-creator, to learn about love and creativity against a backdrop of greed and ego. Ye are gods in training.

The sabbath is a space in your consciousness that can be visited any time and at all times, and where you meet God with love and gratitude. Honor the divine in all things.

28

"I took my place in the world, and I appeared in flesh.
I found all of them intoxicated and none of them thirsty.
So my soul became afflicted for the sons of men, because they are blind in their hearts and do not have sight; for empty they came into the world, and empty too they seek to leave the world. But for the moment they are intoxicated. When they shake off their wine they will repent."

There are those thirsty for spiritual food and drink who are asleep and not awake, and therefore dead to their spiritual nature and consciousness. Incarnation is to be *in carne*, or in the flesh, and humans being are often stuck in the illusion of the reality of the world during an incarnation. They come in empty and they leave empty, never being full and never waking up. They know not their divine natures, and possess a fear of death. In Paradise, all will be revealed to them and without judgment. When they pass over and go into Paradise, they will realize how much they languished but did not nurture themselves nor others. Perhaps then they will choose to reincarnate and come back to awaken and feed the hungry, clothe the naked, care for the sick, bury the dead, give spiritual drink to those who thirst, and sight to those blind to reality. When they awaken, they will seek union and will be alive and free.

29

"If the flesh came into being because of Spirit, it is a wonder. But if Spirit came into being because of the body, then that is a wonder of wonders. I am amazed at how this great wealth has made its home in this poverty."

The soul of each person is a great gift, and free will is its powerful creative tool. The soul with free will dwells in all human creations, and yet they know it not. They live lives out of ignorance of the Spirit in the illusion, and with the sense that there is separation from God. Separation is only an idea—your idea. So change your mind and keep the change.

30

"Where there are three gods, they are gods.
And where there are two or one, I am with him."

I Am that I Am, whether perceived as the One or Many. The Source is the Source, and all is a function of the One—a function of the Light. I have many names and many faces, but one essence and creative beingness.

31

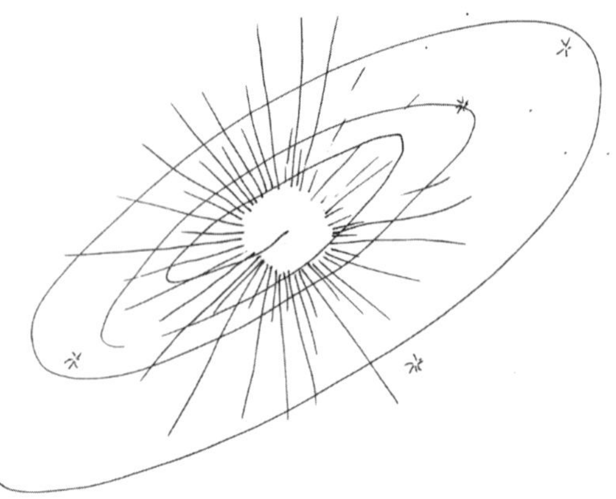

"A prophet is not accepted in his own village,
nor can a physician heal those who know him."

Peers find it challenging to believe in someone whom they believe they know all about. Belief is the key to creation, and your mind is the builder. Therefore, to be healed is to believe in yourself. The healer can be the catalyst, and yet it is you who do the healing from your own divine nature. We are all made of the same One, and capable of loving all, whether a neighbor, a stranger at the gate, or the totality of ourselves.

32

"A city being built on a high mountain with fortification cannot fall, nor can it be hidden."

Live within your high place, your highest self, and you will not falter. Make your light shine from the highest part of your consciousness, and you will be a light to all. Fortify yourself with love and confidence, and stand up when you are called into service. As God calls, respond, "Lord, here am I!"

33

"Preach from your housetops that which you will hear.
For no one lights a lamp and puts it under a bushel,
nor does he put it in a hidden place, but rather he sets it out
so that everyone who enters and leaves will see its light."

Listen to your inner voice, surrender and obey, and be not afraid to let your light, your life, and your consciousness shine. Then your life and your light become an example to all, and you are a way-shower and a guidepost on the path. Teach and heal, with their permission, those who will choose to hear you and see you. Then, as they hear and see you, they will come to know themselves.

34

"If a blind person leads a blind person, both fall into the pit."

If you are not awake, you will attract those who are not awake, for that is the Law of Attraction. The Law of Attraction brings that which is like yourself to you, but also that which is opposite. Therefore, seek that which brings you to the Light, and those who know you in the Light will follow. In this age, as we go forward into the future, only world leaders who are spiritual need be chosen to serve, and then elected. Make it so.

35

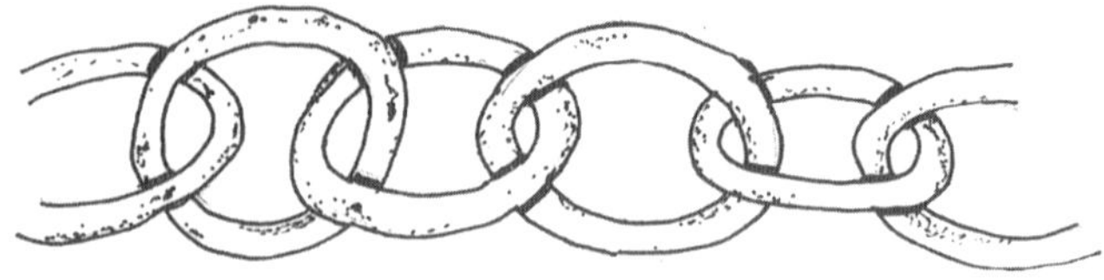

"It is not possible for anyone to enter the house of a strong man and take it by force unless he binds the owner. If he binds the owner, he will (be able to) ransack his house."

A person may say, "There is nothing I can do—my hands are tied." It is their choice now, or from before, and even from previous lives that created this. Respect the free will of every individual. But if they surrender their will to you, then you may be in control, but what karma is in that for both of you? Who is ransacking whom?

36

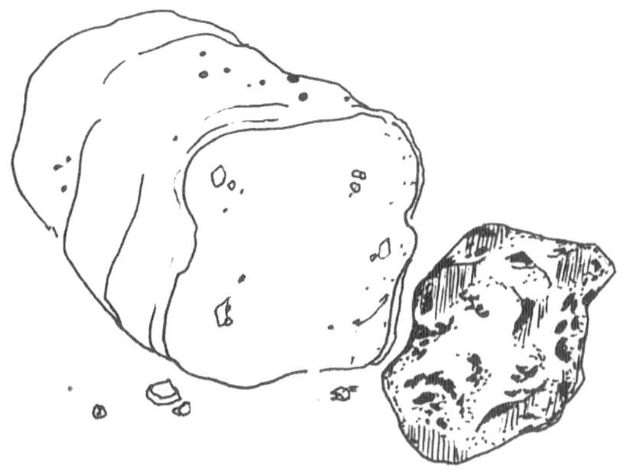

"Do not be concerned about what you will wear."

Do not worry, for worrying actually produces the very thing that you have concerns about, and your fear will bring that event to pass. How can I give you bread if you are holding on to a stone or your hand is clenched in angst? God provides all, and will feed and clothe you and nourish your soul from morning until night, with your consent. Therefore, it is important that you be a good receiver. ("Consider the lilies of the field...")

37

"When you disrobe without being ashamed and place your garments under your feet like little children and tread on them, then (will you see) the son of the living one, and you will not be afraid."

Rise above your nature and conquer your lower self, losing all sense of shame and fear. Your clothes are merely symbols of those thought forms that are your chosen reflection of your ego and personality. Remove those thoughts and ideas and be open—trusting like a little child, full of innocence, expectation, and wonder. For God loves you eternally and without conditions, even the very conditions that you wrap yourself in. So strip yourself of those, love your true nature, and be not ashamed to be a child of God. ("Who told you that you were naked?")

38

"Many times have you desired to hear these words which I am saying to you and you have no one else to hear them from. There will be days when you will look for me and will not find me."

God sends messengers into the world with food for your very soul. Take advantage of a good teacher. Sit down at their feet, hold your tongue and honor them. If your teacher says, "Here am I," then go to them, for the days may be short and the nights too long. Don't put off until tomorrow what you can do today, for tomorrow sees what today decrees.

39

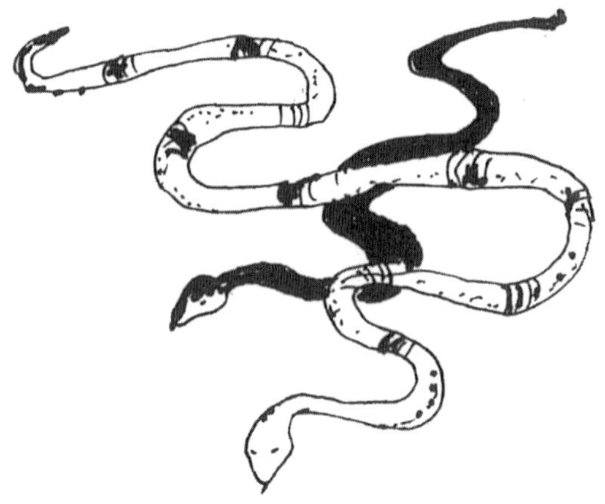

"The Pharisees and the scribes have taken the keys of knowledge (gnosis) and have hidden them. They themselves have not entered, nor have they allowed to enter, those who want to. You, however, be as wise as serpents and as innocent as doves."

Do not give your power away; don't allow yourself to be put off by those who would deny you access to knowledge and wisdom. (If you walk among snakes, wear snake boots!) You have every right to the gifts of the Spirit and to mastership of your own self. Trust your own spiritual nature, listen to your still small voice, and obey.

40

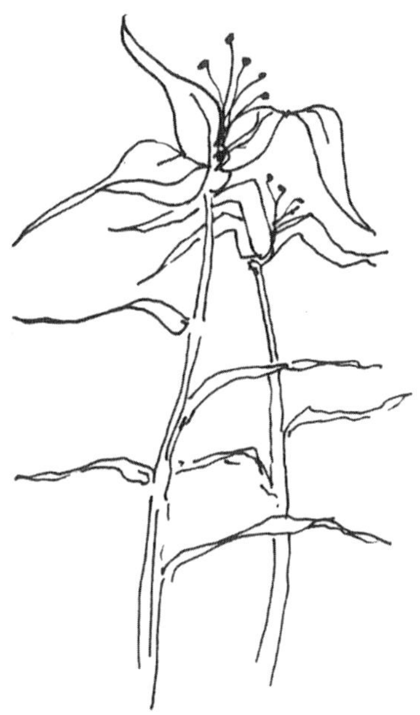

"A grapevine has been planted outside the Father, and being unsound it will be pulled up by its roots and destroyed."

Before you were born, you created the opportunity to flourish in life. Put yourself into good soil, weed and water your garden, and turn your face toward the sun, keeping your connection to your higher power. Grow where you are planted. You were planted where you are by your own divine guidance.

41

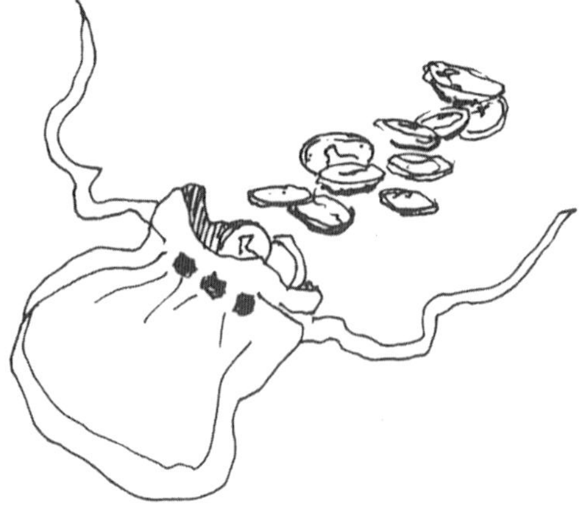

"He who has something in his hand will receive more, and he who has nothing will be deprived of even the little he has."

When you realize the power you have to create, you will be a natural creator. You have always had this ability but were simply not aware of it, nor of its possible consequences. Like attracts like and is a law of manifestation. Therefore, if you conceive of yourself as impoverished, you will create poverty, and I congratulate you on your ability to be a Master of Poverty. Now turn it around and become a Master of Abundance. The key to success in manifestation is your power of unconditional self-love coupled with your willingness to be a receiver.

42

"Become passers-by."

Being a passer-by means observing what is on the spiritual path. Everything on the path is significant, as there are no accidents nor coincidences. As you pass by, observe what has been and what is, and what has been created by you as a significant signpost on your spiritual journey. Be keen to observe the things of your dreams. (As mammals we have between four and seven dreams a night.) Lucid dreaming is the ability to be aware that you are dreaming while you are dreaming, and even directing the dream as it unfolds. So be awake in your dreams and of what you have created and are now creating, for dreams foreshadow your awakened state. When you pass over and have your life review, you will remember all of the dreams that you have ever had and know what they mean. During your life review one of the questions that Spirit will ask you is, "What did you choose to learn from the time in the earth plane that I gave you?"

43

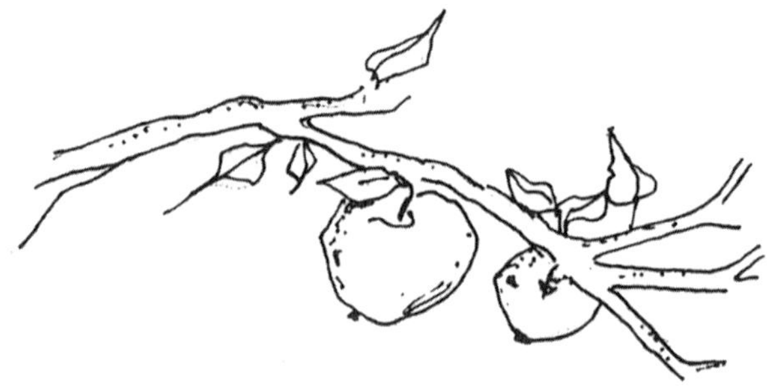

"You do not realize who I am from what I say to you, but you have become like the Jews, for they (either) love the tree and hate the fruit (or) love the fruit and hate its tree."

By what authority do you do or say these things? What is the source? How may I trust that?

You shall know them by the results of their labors: the "fruit of the tree" will be your evidence. Some know not love nor will they permit themselves to be loved. Those who do not love themselves will not permit themselves to know God. If you resent the ultimate love, you may reject and/or choose not to hear the bearer of the Truth of Love; you may reject the source of the Truth or the witness to the Truth. If you have seen me, you have seen the Father, who has sent me. I am as constant at the stars and as steadfast as the rainbow as given to Noah—a covenant, a contract between me and thee.

"If you blaspheme against the Father, you will be forgiven,
and if you blaspheme against the Son, you will be forgiven.
But whosoever blasphemes against the Holy Spirit
will not be forgiven, neither on Earth nor in Heaven."

The thought forms Father and Son are human concepts limited in their own natures. However, Holy Spirit, or neutrinos, which is unconditional love and the glue of the universe, is the "I AM" of creation. In concert with the Law of Cause and Effect, or karma, doubting the Creator reaps its own rewards, so don't kick against the thorns. Out of your own mouth will come the very thing to bite the Source (you), and it does not come from God.

45

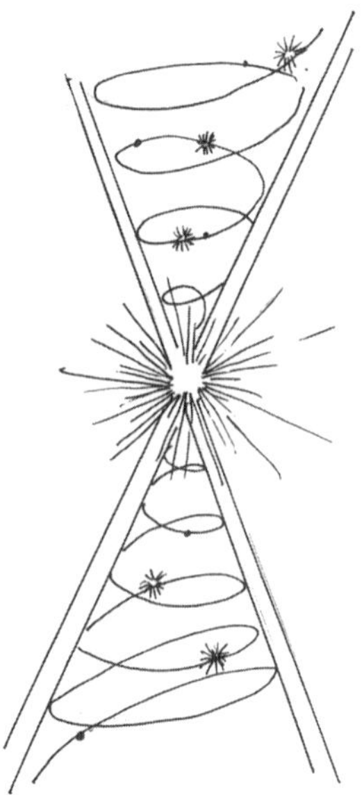

"Grapes are not harvested from thorns, and figs are not gathered from thistles, for they do not produce fruit. A good man brings forth good from his storehouse, while an evil man brings forth evil things from his evil storehouse, which is in his heart, and says evil things. Out of the abundance of the heart, he brings forth evil things."

It is not what you put in your mouth that corrupts you, but rather the words that you speak. From the perfect past, the present moment, and the perfect future, thoughts become manifest. A good seed produces good fruit. Therefore, observe what you do, and that is how you will know what power you have exhibited.

46

"Among those born of women, from Adam to John the Baptist, there is no one so superior to John that his eyes should not be lowered (before him). Yet, as I have said, whichever one of you comes to be a child will be acquainted with the Kingdom and will become superior to John."

Innocence restored brings the Kingdom: unconditional self-love karmically brings all. Each person has the potential for self-realization—Buddhahood, Christhood. Realize your full potential. Forgive, release, let go and step into your Mastership.

47

"It is impossible for a man to mount two horses or to stretch two bows at the same time. Likewise, it is impossible for a servant to serve two masters, for he will honor one and treat the other contemptuously. No man drinks old wine and immediately desires to drink new wine. And new wine is not put into old wineskins, lest they burst; nor is old wine put into a new wineskin, lest it be spoiled. An old patch is not sewn into a new garment because a tear would result."

A new life and different perspective is not able to be contained in the old house of your old consciousness. Becoming aware, enlightened, or ordained is like new wine. There is more gold in your aura, and it may cause old friends and old habits to fall away, allowing new friends and new life styles more compatible with the new you to appear. The Law of Attraction is always active and is governed by your mind and thoughts.

48

"If two make peace with each other in one house,
they will say to the mountain,
'Move away,' and it will move away."

Here we speak of the polarization of opposites in the earth plane, the yin and yang within each of us in this dimension. When you become one through enlightenment, you embrace the whole—a merger of the opposites for balance. With these combined, you can take on major obstacles and they will be set aside. So forgive, release, and let go, for there is power and total compassion in loving all of your true nature, and thereby embracing the divine within.

49

"Blessed are the solitary and elect—you shall find the Kingdom. For you are from it, and to it you will return."

Exercise your free will to be chosen. Being chosen may put you on a path of an alone (all one) situation in your mind and in your life. But you were chosen, and you chose, before your birth, and now in your life you must use your free will to accept what you have already committed yourself to complete. Choosing to honor your contract puts you in a state of The Kingdom, or Grace. In this be grateful, for you have returned to your full self.

50

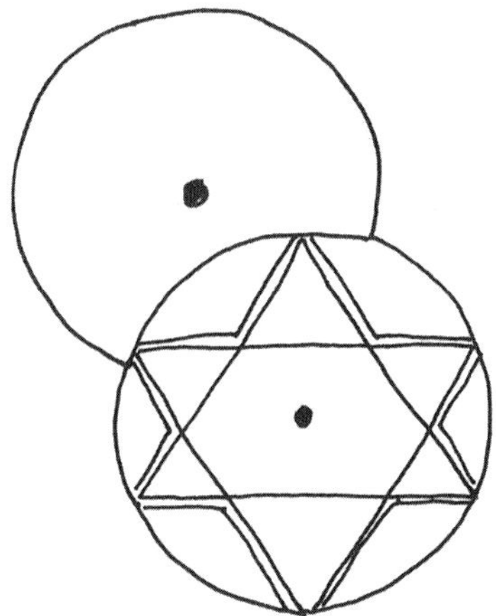

"If they ask you, 'Where did you come from?,' answer them, 'We came from the light— the place where the light came into being of its own accord and established itself and became manifest through its image.' If they ask you, 'Is it you?,' say,'We are its children, and we are the elect of the living Father.' If they say to you, 'What is the sign of your Father in you?,' say to them, 'It is movement and repose.' "

A quality of the Light is motion—movement. And yet the Light's origin is the stillness before movement—in the void before the Big Bang, before Light was created from the love from God. I AM brings creation and the eternal evolution of the One in *all* its forms. Aspects of the One, or functions of that Light, are "children of the Light." Then on the seventh day God rested.

51

"What you are looking forward to has already come, but you do not recognize it."

Grace is omnipresent. It is the acceptance of unconditional love in your life. It is always available to you, even if you are not aware of it. Choosing separation through free will and ignorance does not allow you to perceive it, and yet it is there. The Kingdom is unconditional love. The new world is already here, for it is within, above you, beneath you, and all around you; it is all-pervasive, yet you may not know it nor see it. When you choose to love yourself as God does, unconditionally, all will be restored to you in the blink of an eye.

52

"You have omitted the one (prophet) living in your presence, and have spoken (only) of the dead."

Avoid looking to the way-showers of old—there is a presence in the present, and it doesn't require a prophecy. All is happening now and is available to you in the now. Today is the result of all of your yesterdays. Look to today for the realization of the present moment and the foreshadowing of the probable future. In that future will still reside the One speaking to the many of the remembrance of being with God.

53

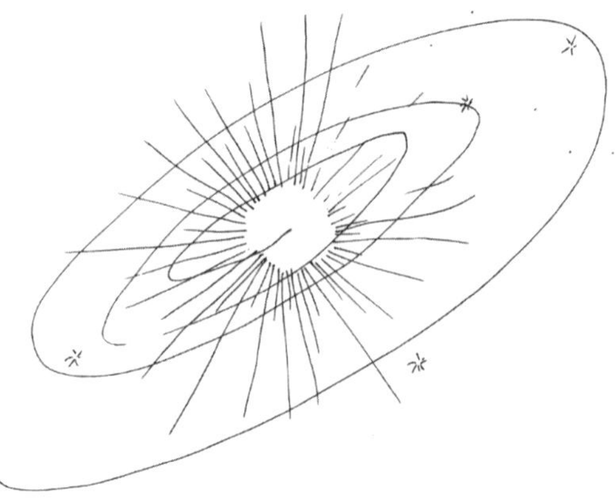

"If it (circumcision) were beneficial, their Father would have beget them already circumcised. Rather, the true circumcision in Spirit has become completely profitable."

Circumcision is a sacrifice of the heart. It is the willingness to give that part of self in acknowledgment of that which gave you life, not as a piece of flesh but a true part of your nature. Circumcision is a gesture of a remembered contract and, as such, is not a requirement of the flesh, but of the Spirit. As you give of your free will back to God, you allow that part of you to become one again with the One. Abraham's symbol is not necessary in the physical reality. Make your sacrifice (to make sacred) in your heart—willingly, lovingly, and in the Spirit.

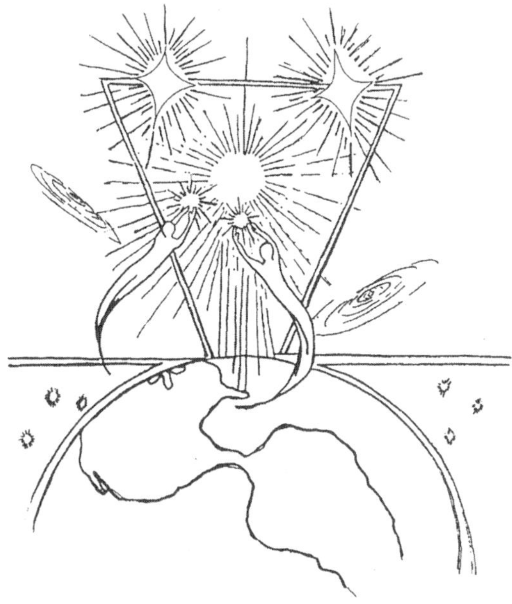

54

"Blessed are the poor, for theirs is the Kingdom of Heaven."

The poor create their own poverty, sometimes from lifetimes before, and also from not allowing themselves to receive and to give. Poverty is created out of ignorance in this life, but may have been willingly chosen in the time before this life as a way of finding balance and harmony. When they return to the Light, they will know the true riches of life. Still, they must allow themselves to receive their good. "The poor, you will have with you always," but only until they use their free will and choose to receive love. All is love in all of its forms.

55

"Whosoever does not hate his father and his mother cannot become my disciple. And whosoever does not hate his brothers and sisters and take up his cross in my way is not worthy of me."

God must come first in your life and in all things. Even before father and mother, brother and sister, wife and husband and children. God is the author of all of those lives. The cross is a burden of Light that may put you at odds with all. Yet, be steadfast, and God will honor you for your patience and persistence in love.

56

"Whosoever has come to understand the world found only a corpse, and whosoever found a corpse is superior to the world."

The world is a matrix of energies, a superstructure, a framework, and a school for spiritual learning. The true value of the world—as part of God's body, as part of the whole, as a living entity—is to be known. Know her and respect the beings in and of her, both visible and invisible. All things are sacred, from the smallest to the greatest. You are greater than the world, and you are charged with being stewards of her.[1]

---

1 "And God blessed them, and God said to them, "Be fruitful and multiply, and fill the earth and tame it; and have stewardship of the fish of the sea and of the birds of the air and of every living thing that moves upon the earth."

—*Genesis 1:28*

57

"The Kingdom of the Father is like a man who had (good) seed, and his enemy came in the night and sowed weeds among the good seed. The man did not allow the weeds to pulled up; he said, 'I am afraid that you will go intending to pull up the weeds and pull up the wheat along with them.' For on the day of the harvest, the weeds will be plainly visible, and then they will be pulled up and burned."

Your life path is your "garden." The enemy is within in the form of ignorance, and manifests itself in your free-will choices. With the Law of Cause and Effect, all is revealed in your life review, if not sooner. The good you do, and all else, is winnowed out in your life-review process, and you will judge yourself. "What have you done with the life that I gave you?" is a question to by answered by you when you pass over.

58

"Blessed are they who have suffered and found life."

Rejoice and be delighted in your pursuit of self-realization and enlightenment. The slings and arrows of life's challenges are as nothing compared to the Kingdom.

59

"Take heed of the living one while you are alive,
lest when you die and seek to see him you are unable to do so."

Physical death does not mean that you attain instant enlightenment. You continue to seek to know and understand. There is only life and levels of awareness, which change according to the knowledge and experiences you gain. So seek the One always.

60

"Look for a place for yourselves within repose, lest you become a corpse and be eaten."

A place to rest, or of repose, is a place of comprehension, understanding, and contentment. Seek this, otherwise you may consume yourself with "ill ease." In choosing not to love yourself you create dis-ease and discontentment. You may argue for your lack, and convince yourself of unworthiness, but these are just ideas based on ignorance of the Truth. Remember, if you argue strong enough for your limitations you get to keep them.

61

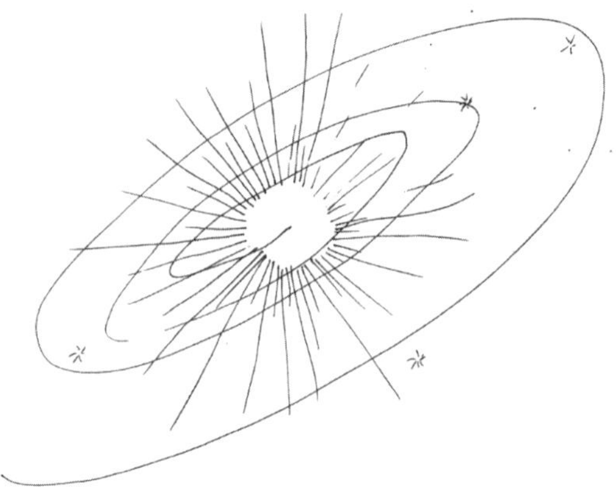

"Two will rest on a bed, and one will die and the other will live."... "I am he who exists from the undivided. I was given some of the things of my Father."... "Therefore, I say, if he is destroyed he will be filled with light, but if he is divided he will be filled with darkness."

Be not divided from Self nor from the One by choice or by ignorance. I am one who comes from what is whole, and so must you know it and be One.

62

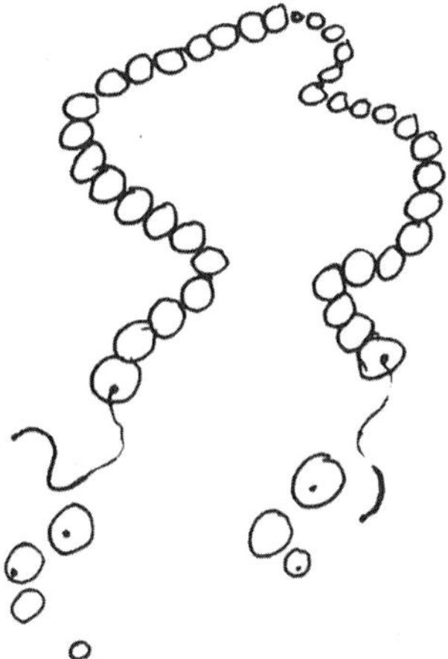

"To those who are worthy of my mysteries I tell my mysteries. Do not let your left hand know what your right hand is doing."

Avoid being opposite from your true divine nature. Be whole and be worthy. The left and right hands have their functions, and it's best when they work together. Your consciousness and awareness are like fine gems to be valued. Therefore, avoid putting yourself in harm's way, nor in front of others who do not value your awareness and cannot see the beauty of it. "Do not cast pearls before swine."

63

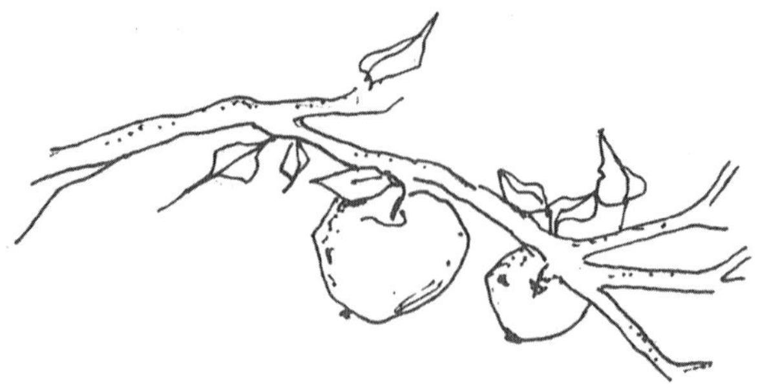

"There was a rich man who had much money. He said, 'I shall put my money to use so that I may sow, reap, plant, and fill my storehouse with produce, and I shall lack nothing.' These were his intentions, but that same night he died. Let him who has ears hear."

Enjoy the fruits of your labor, both in giving and in receiving love in the present moment. Do not put off until tomorrow what you can create consciously today. Be in the present and out of wholeness create tomorrow today. "Tomorrow sees what today decrees."

64

"A man had received visitors. When he had prepared the dinner, he sent his servant to invite the guests. The servant went to the first one and said, ' My master invites you.' But he answered, 'I have claims against some merchants. They are coming to me this evening. I must go and give them my orders. I ask to be excused from the dinner.' The servant went to another and said to him, 'My master has invited you.' He answered, 'I have just bought a house and am required for the day. I shall not have any spare time.' The servant went to another and said to him, 'My master invites you.' He answered, 'My friend is going to get married, and I am to prepare the banquet. I shall not be able to come. I ask to be excused from the dinner.' He went to another and said to him, 'My master invites you.' The guest said to him, 'I have just bought a farm, and I am on my way to collect the rent. I shall not be able to come. I ask to be excused.' The servant returned and said to his master, 'Those whom you invited to the dinner have asked to be excused.' The master said to his servant, 'Go outside to the streets and bring back those whom you happen to meet, so that they may dine.' Businessmen and merchants will not enter the place of my Father."

Know what is truly valuable to you in the present moment, realizing that there are no accidents nor coincidences. Come when you are called by the One. Answer the call to service at the point of the call. There is no time and space for procrastination. Act in the moment and answer the call to action.

65

"There was a good man who owned a vineyard. He leased it to tenant farmers so that they would work it and he would collect produce from them. He sent his servant so that the tenants might give him the produce. The tenant farmers seized his servant and beat him, all but killing him. The servant went back and told his master. The master said, 'Perhaps he did not recognize them.' He sent another servant. The tenants beat this one as well. Then the owner sent his son and said, 'Perhaps they will show respect to my son.' Because the tenants knew that it was he who was the heir to the vineyard, they seized him and killed him. Let him who has ears hear."

Ego and greed are the shadows of this world, but all is God's and all is of God. You are charged with being a steward of the planet and that is all. You come in with nothing and you leave with nothing—except the memories of your thoughts and deeds. What, then, can you truly possess? I sent my own son into the vineyard, and they knew him not and killed him. I created him, and he went willingly into the field to bring in a great harvest. But they knew him not, nor would they know the One who sent him. ("If you have seen me, you have seen the Father." "Whatever you do to these, the least of my brethren, you do unto me.")

66

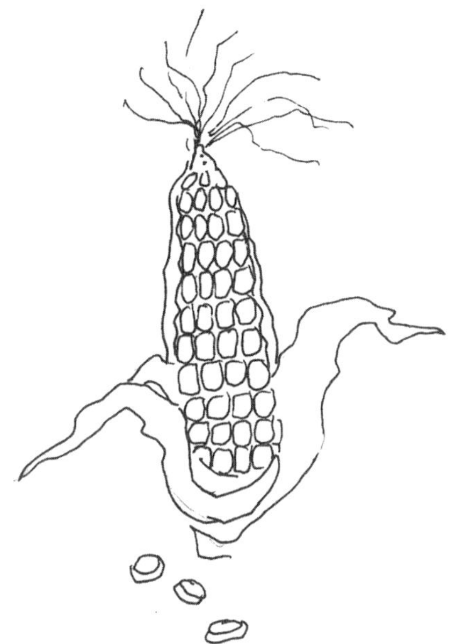

"Show me the stone that the builders have rejected. That one is the cornerstone."

Everyone is loved unconditionally by God. A person loved by God and rejected by others can then be the very foundation of a new creation of this world. When all realize egalitarianism and the good it brings, and that all are worthy, then the cornerstone is laid. In the Priesthood of Melchizedek[1] are many who would have been rejected by their own churches and religions, and yet each one is a power for transformation and the very seed for growth in a new age.

1 The teachings of Melchizedek—a totally balanced, authoritative incarnation of Christ prior to that of Jesus—on topics such as reincarnation, spiritual development, and free will, are presented in this manual that relates a positive approach to the current transitional stage of spiritual evolution.

Chesbro, Daniel and James Erickson. *The Order of Melchizedek: Love, Willing Service, and Fulfillment*. Forres, Scotland: Findhorn Press, 2010.

67

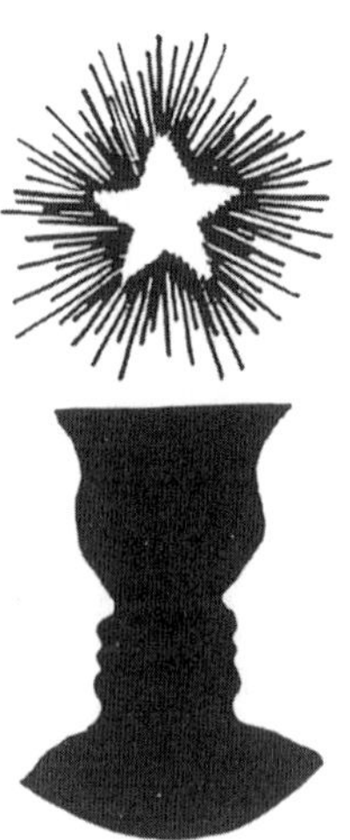

"If one who knows the all still feels personal deficiency, he is completely deficient."

Academic knowledge is empty and street smarts are useless if you do not unconditionally love yourself and have compassion for all others. Academic knowledge and street smarts are merely a reflection of an illusion of self-knowing—the evolution of creation understood at a moment. I look in a mirror dimly, but now I see face to face, and the old things have passed away. These three abide: Faith, Hope, and Charity, but the greatest of these is Love and Compassion.

68

"Blessed are you when you are hated and persecuted.
Whenever you have been persecuted they will find no place."

It may be in your spiritual contract to be persecuted and to teach a lesson thereby. Persecution is energy directed at you unjustly. It returns to the persecutor, creator of the persecution, and is magnified in karma to the one who created it. The Universe will reward you for the energy that you experienced. Then be mindful to resist revenge, for it creates its own end also. ("Thou cannot kick against the thorns…")

69

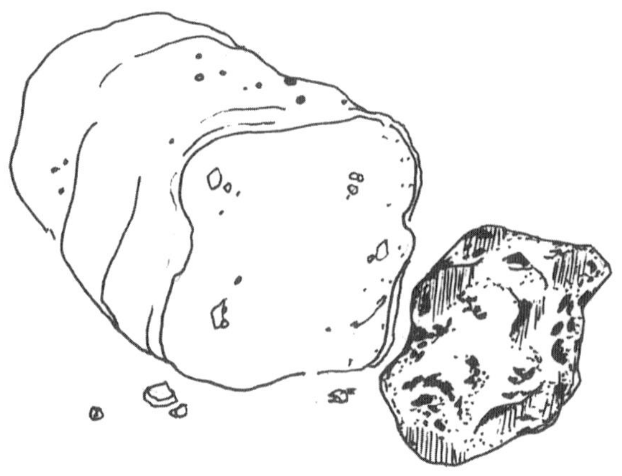

"Blessed are they that have been persecuted within themselves,
for it is they who have truly come to know the Father.
Blessed are the hungry, for they who desire will be filled."

Your life review will show the results of your resistance to revenge. Resist revenge and use compassion to whatever degree is "God like." Ask for what you need and it is granted, and therefore be a good receiver. Hunger for anything and be filled, for the Law of Cause and Effect prevails.

70

"That which you have will save you when you bring it forth from yourselves. That which you do not have within you will kill you when you do not have it within you."

What you have within you is great, that is, your free will, for it is equal to God in power. It is never true that this power is not within you—it is! But if you believe that it is not there, then you cannot access it fully, and the end of that may be your physical body's death. Death and darkness are lack of enlightenment and are equal to ignorance. Ignorance is the lack of knowledge either by choice or circumstance. Either action or lack of action involving a person, situation, or event can be a form of ignorance.

71

"I will destroy this house and no one will be able to build it (up again)."

In a previous life Jesus was Melchizedek, king of Ur and Salem. Those two places later became Jerusalem. Jesus is describing two things: the termination of his physical body and the temple in Jerusalem, and only God could reconstruct a temple of that stature, whether physical or spiritual. The destruction of "this house" signaled the end of the old age and the beginning of the next. The third temple is within you and is not made of stone and mortar but of flesh and blood and the Spirit.

72

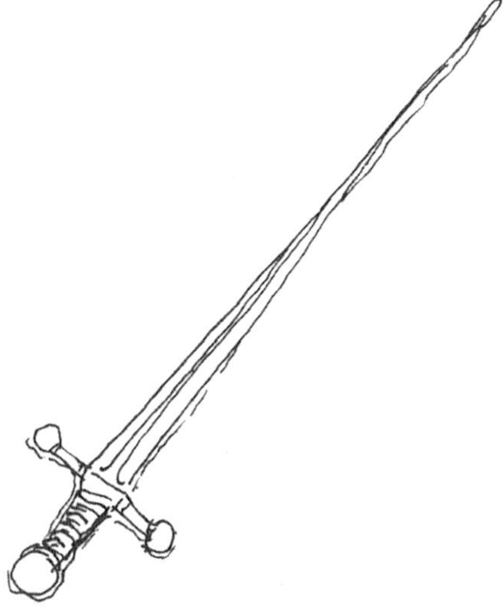

"I am not a divider, am I?"

Jesus, being God, is Oneness. However, His teachings may cause division—the division of thought. Father against son, mother against daughter, spouse against spouse, and yet, in Truth, all are One. Though at odds in thought, the higher self or soul knows the Truth of Oneness. ("I do not come to bring peace, but a sword…")

73

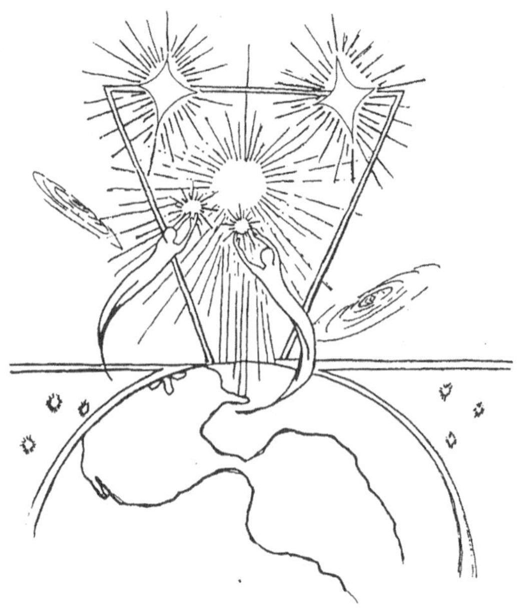

"The harvest is great but the laborers are few.
Ask the lord, therefore, to send out laborers to the harvest."

The harvest is the coming of the new age of Aquarius and the gleaning of the effects of the Great Transformation. Ask to receive more souls of free will to help in the harvest.

74

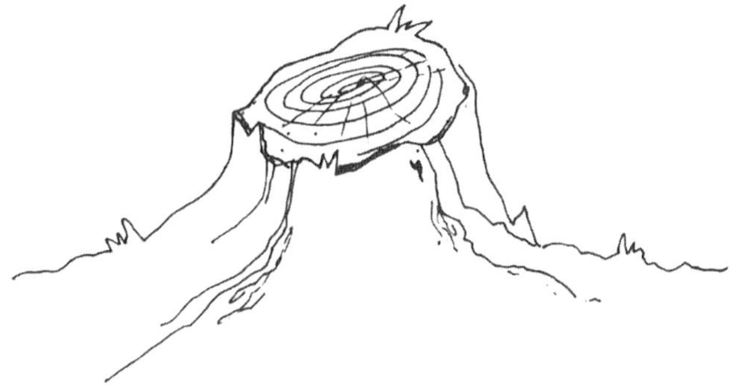

"There are many around the drinking trough,
but there is nothing in the cistern."

Many will follow the empty words and deeds of a few. They stay and cling to these words, even though nothing of any substance is available. In so doing, they give away their power. So ask, "What are the first fruits of their labor?" If there is no fruit on the tree, cut it down and go to another.

75

"Many are standing without the door,
but it is the solitary who will enter the bridal chamber."

"The solitary" represents the single vision of Oneness. This perception, often from intuition, and/or perhaps the third eye (the single eye), requires focus. The wedding chamber is where merger takes place—the union of the soul, mind, and body—and celebration follows. Focus on your Oneness.

"The Kingdom of the Father is like a merchant who had a consignment of merchandise and then discovered a pearl. The merchant was shrewd, for he sold the merchandise and bought the pearl alone for himself. You, too, seek His unfailing and enduring treasure where no moth comes near to devour and no worm destroys."

Spend your energy in the pursuit of Truth, Wisdom and Oneness. Once found, these become a thing of great value to your soul. Do not cast it before the ignorant or those blind to Spirit, lest they destroy it. Keep that which is holy locked in your heart and in your mind, knowing that nothing can take from you nor destroy your awakening without your permission.

77

"It is I who am the Light above them all. It is I who am the All. From me they all come forth, and unto me did the All extend. Split a piece of wood, and I am there. Lift up the stone, and you will find me there."

Oneness permeates all of creation and, indeed, is all of creation. I Am All in All. There is no place where I Am is not. Everything possesses a spark of the divine within, as a twin flame to the One. There is only God and there is only Good.

78

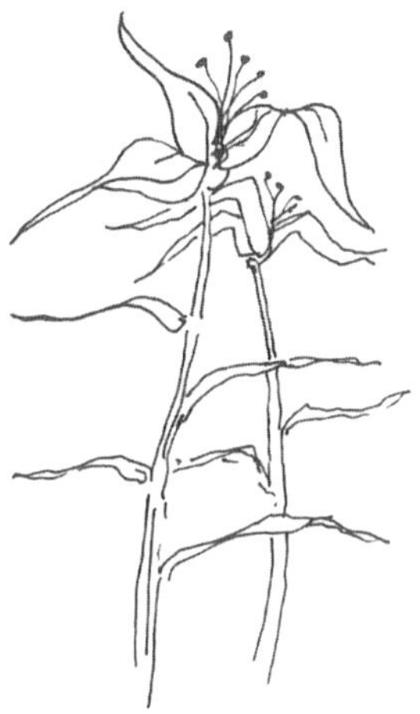

"Why did you come out into the desert? To see a reed shaken by the wind? To see a man clothed in fine garments like your kings and your great men? Upon them are the fine garments but they are unable to discern the Truth."

What are you seeking? Appearances can be deceiving. Those who seem to have it all may not, both in how they are seen and in what they may appear to represent. Even so, there is Truth in everything, and if what they say helps you to get through the day, so be it. ("Consider the lilies of the field...")

79

"Blessed are those who have heard the word of the Father and have truly kept it. There will be days when you will say, 'Blessed is the womb which has not conceived and the breasts which have not given milk.' "

Times are coming when you may be glad that there was no one to suckle—times of war, adversities, and natural calamities. In that moment it may seem a perception of imbalance, but all is God and all is Good. And what shall you do with travail? Feed the hungry, bandage the wounded, and preach Oneness. For all are One, and adversity sometimes brings us to see our family through the turmoil. Blessed are you and the mother for recognizing Godness and Oneness.

80

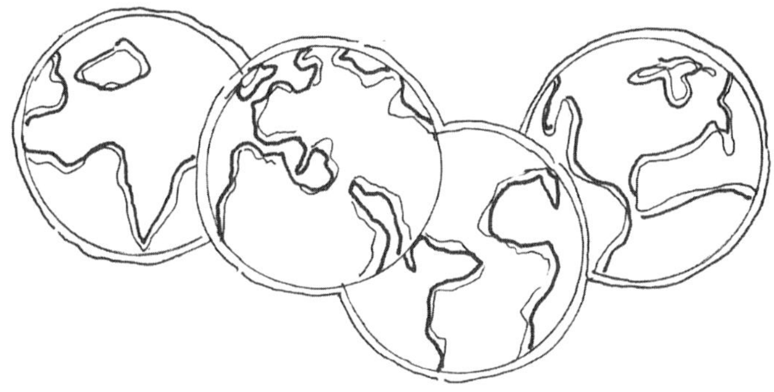

"He who has recognized the world has found the body, and he who has found the body is superior to the world."

The body is limited in and to its senses, and it reacts to its environment. To truly seek to know is to discover and uncover what is the greater Truth. So it is useful to recognize what is beyond your senses to the greater reality. The world is merely a school for the soul's development. Therefore, avoid getting caught in the appearance of the illusion, but remain in gratitude for its beauty as a part of the body of God. ("Those who have eyes to see, let them see.") Then know that before the world was I Am, and so are you in the Spirit.

81

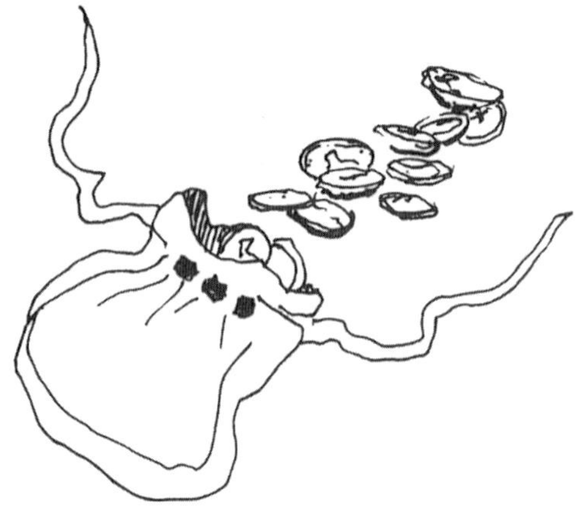

"Let him who has grown rich be king,
but let him who possesses power renounce it."

Wealth here does not refer to acquired things, but rather means an abundançe of the gifts of Spirit, Love, Compassion, and Charity. Proper rule is being compassionate and taking care of all with their consent. The only true and correct use of power is service to others, so power without compassion is potentially dangerous. God is all of the power that there truly is.

82

"He who is near me is near the fire,
but he who is far from me is far from the Kingdom."

Fire is a source for light, and it symbolizes awareness and enlightenment. Fire transforms, purifies, illuminates, and dispels the darkness. The Sun, and all of the suns of God, produce neutrinos, which are unconditional love, both seen and unseen—the Holy Spirit. Using your free will you may choose to not go near the fire. In so choosing, a person will be far from the Truth, and therefore farther from the Kingdom, or the Source, or the means to access it. There is one who will baptize with fire *and* with the Holy Spirit.

83

"The images are made manifest to man, but the light in them remains concealed in the image of the Light of the Father. He will become manifest, but His image will remain concealed by His Light."

We are made in the image and likeness of God—of the Light. But our senses don't show us this awareness, and without awareness and knowledge we only see the outer. The inner is the ultimate reflection of the outer, and the outer is a reflection of the inner. ("As above, so below.") God is the Light, and His image is light and not in body or form. It is pure and unconditional Love in the expression of light. From the One come the many, and they continue to evolve forever, both visible and invisible.

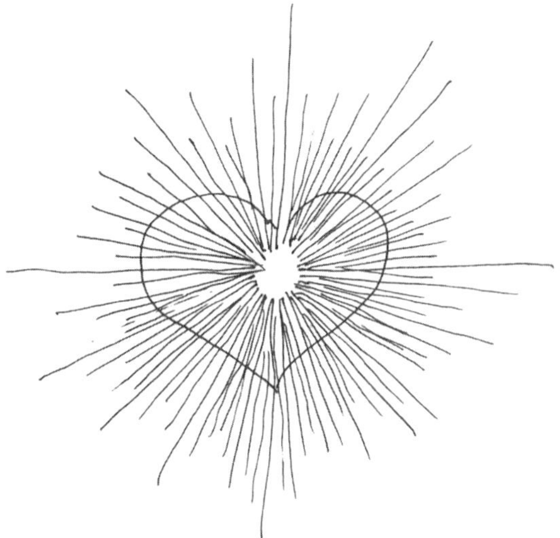

"When you see your likeness you rejoice. But when you see your images, which came into being before you, those which neither die nor become manifest, how much you will have to bear!"

See yourself in the present moment as the divine being that you truly are. As you become aware of your past and past lives, and become aware of the future probabilities, how will you deal with that? Know that in all things there is perfection, and what you may soon perceive is also perfection.

85

"Adam came into being from a great power and a great wealth, but he did not become worthy of you. Had he been worthy, he would not have experienced death."

Adam, an expression of God the Light, came to serve the human condition. He lost his focus in separation, using his free will: he recognized separation and the illusion of death was his reward. ("Who told you that you were naked?")

86

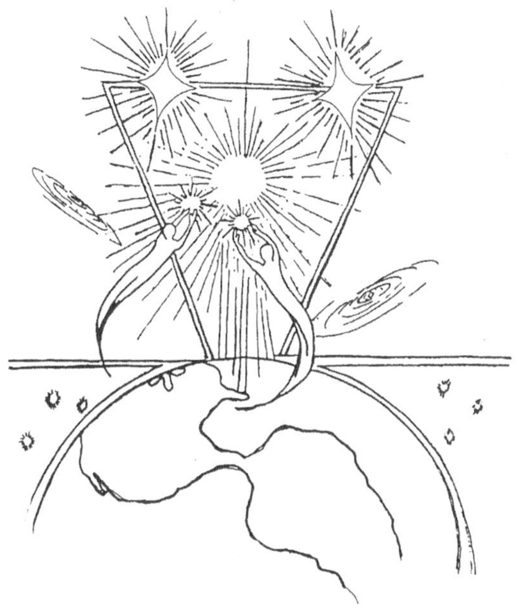

"The foxes have their holes, the birds have their nests, but the son of man has no place to lay his head and rest."

A prophet may not be recognized in their own land, and thus they have nowhere to rest their head. Where do we belong? We are part mammal and part Spirit, and where is our home? Our animal nature has animal instincts, and our spiritual nature has spiritual sense and intuitions. Yet it may be that the messengers of God go unrecognized, persecuted, and even executed. The place for them to rest their head is at the breast of God and in the Light.

87

"Wretched is the body that is dependent only upon a body, and wretched is the soul that is dependent on these two."

How miserable are you if you only depend on your physical body for senses, and do not connect with the Spirit that dwells within you. If a person depends only on their body they are depending on a very limited and limiting device. Likewise, the person who believes that their happiness depends on someone else is self-fooled and then disappointed. And if the soul only depends on the body, listening only to the body's senses, it is a shallow thing. Rather, the soul in connection to the Higher Source feeds the mind (the builder) and heart of the body, which in turn feeds the physical body and raises it up. When you love yourself as God loves you, life can be full both in body and in Spirit.

88

"The angels and the prophets will come to you and give you those things you already have. And you give them those things that you have, and say to yourselves, 'When will they come and take what is theirs?' "

The teacher reminds you of what is yours by divine right and encourages you to accept it. They give you insight, perhaps, into the probable futures and glimpses into Truth. They may share with you their ignorance as well—a half-truth, and limited understanding and actions based on that. Sometimes the eyes cannot accept the simplest gift, for what you have to give them is Love and Acceptance. All of us are both teachers and students of one another.

89

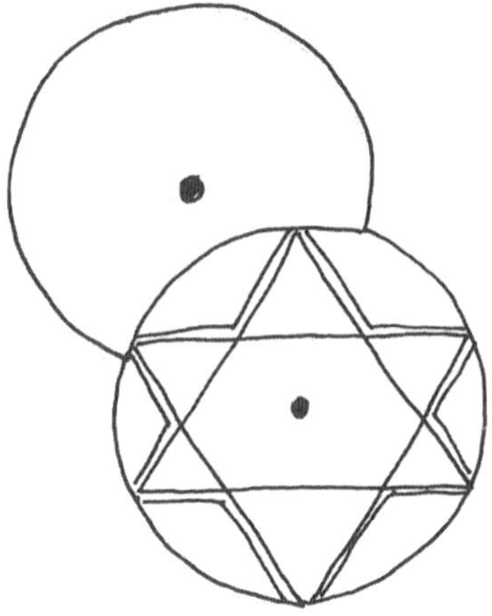

"Why do you wash the outside of the cup?
Don't you realize that He who made the inside
is the same One who made the outside?"

Why only labor over the outer part of understanding—over the obvious? Clear and clean the inner as well. The outer is the inner, and the inner is the outer, and all are One, and One is not without the other, and all are holy.

90

"Come to me, for my yoke is easy and my Lordship is mild, and you will find repose for yourselves."

That which you take on from God is unconditional self-love, and this yoke is to pull you through life and the mastery of your whole self in Love. In Love, we are to serve our sisters and brothers with their consent, and truly, this is not difficult. Rest in the Love of God: enjoy, celebrate, and have fun. May your burdens be light.

91

"You read the face of the sky and the earth,
but you do not recognize the One who is before you,
and you do not know how to read this moment."

You look at astrology, gematria, numerology, phrenology, and all the rest, and yet do not recognize that part of God sent to serve you, and that the design of all these signs shows a possible way to self-fulfillment. Have you not seen signs and wonders and not realized how these things were sent to you from God with foretelling? Look also within, and trust to know that we are One and that God Is.

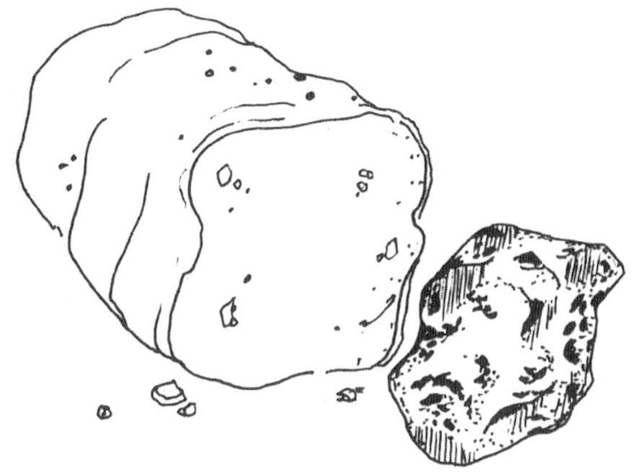

"Seek and you will find. Yet, what you asked me about in former times, and which I did not tell you, I now desire to tell, but you do not inquire after it."

The Master said: "I am willing to tell you the all of God and the wonders of the Universe. It is what you were seeking. But now you no longer ask, and I cannot give you what you no longer ask for." God cannot interfere in your life and free-will decisions without your consent. Your responsibility is to open your heart and ask. ("How can I give you bread when you grasp a stone in your hand?")

93

"Do not give to dogs what is holy,
lest they throw them on the dung heap.
Do not throw pearls to swine..."

Keep what is sacred in your heart and treasure it, for ignorance will not know what to do with Truth, nor know how to handle it. With their permission—and respecting their free will—educate and teach, that they might come to know Truth and honor it.

94

"He who seeks to find, and he who knocks will be admitted."

All operate within the Law of Cause and Effect. For those who seek or take action toward an event, know that it will return and present itself to you. Knock to open the door, and when it is opened go within. Though the latch for the door be on the inside, only you can open it.

95

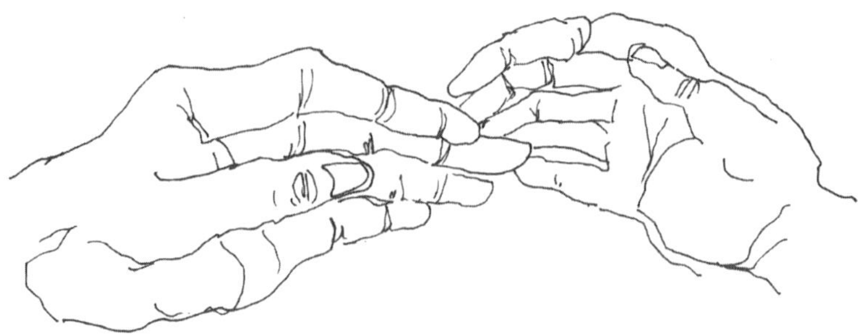

"If you have money do not lend it at interest,
rather give it to one from whom you will not get it back."

Avoid giving with the expectation of a return, for then you will disappoint yourself when nothing is returned. In Truth, a gift with strings attached is not a gift. Rather, give freely, and the Universe, which abounds with abundance, will reward you freely. Of course, this demands that you be a good receiver. Sometimes a former enemy can become your benefactor. If this happens, never let pride and/or a lack of forgiveness get in the way of Love. This is an opportunity for both reconciliation and for you to practice receiving in Love.

96

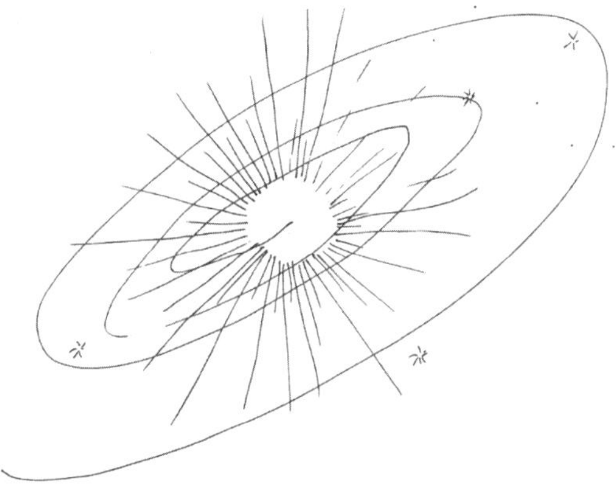

"The Kingdom of the Father is like a woman who took a little leaven, concealed it in some dough, and made it into large loaves. Let him who has ears hear."

The "yeast" is the spark of God in all things ,and it goes where it will. Those of free will allow it to shine and to grow. Those of ignorance never tap into its power and so feel empty. You can never be empty when you choose to not to be. God is the fullness of all things.

97

"The Kingdom of the Father is like a certain woman who was carrying a jar full of meal. While she was walking on the road and still some distance from home, the handle of the jar broke and the meal emptied behind her on the road. She did not realize it, for she had noticed no accident. When she reached her house, she set the jar down and found it empty."

God pours Himself out on all living things. He goes where He will. Those of free will use Him as they will, in ignorance or in the light of understanding, unless they never tap into it and thereby feel empty. You can never be empty unless you choose to believe you are, for God creates all, and is All, and is the source of all things, visible and invisible. You are the jar on the potter's wheel, and God is the potter. But God is also the wheel *and* the clay, and by your desire (and using your free will) you are filled or empty. However, it is just an idea, so therefore choose to be filled. Now look behind you, and see where you have been. Look at your feet, and see where you are. And look ahead, to see where you are going. For God pours Himself out.

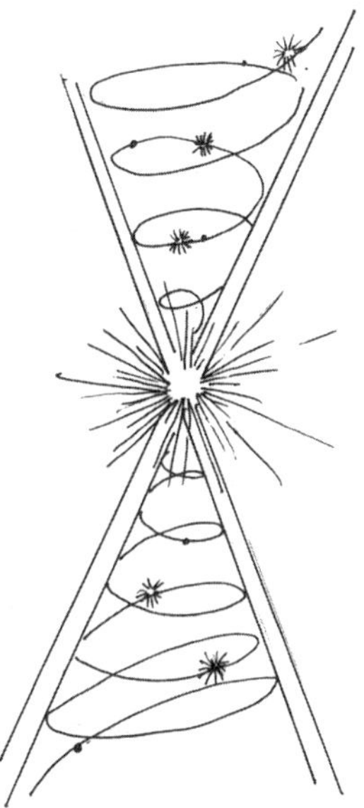

"The Kingdom of the Father is like a certain man who wanted to kill a powerful person. In his own house, he drew his sword and stuck it into the wall in order to find out whether his hand could carry through. Then he slew the powerful man."

What is the process of your intentions? Knowing that imagination and dreams lead to fruition in life, what can you imagine you have the power to achieve? Can you draw your own sword and carry through with the slaying of your illusions? It is neither good nor bad, but just is. In your life review, here is one of the questions to be answered: "What did you do with the life I gave you?" God is the only power that there is, so use your gift of free will wisely, and love openly.

99

"Those who do the will of my Father are my Brothers and my Mother. It is they who will enter the Kingdom of my Father."

The Master spoke of his mother and brothers, and we are no greater than anyone who does the will of God, for we are all brothers and sisters in God. My mother and brothers are no greater than anyone who seeks to find, and when they do find are masters of themselves and servants to all. Live in the Truth, and it shall set you free. "Who is my brother? Who is my sister?"

100

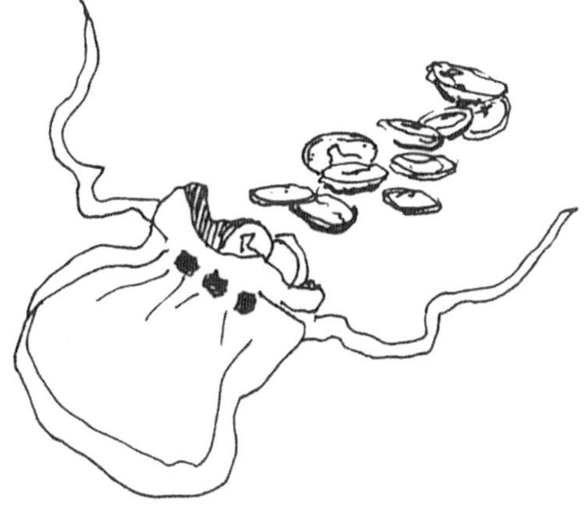

"Give to Caesar what belongs to Caesar, and give to God what belongs to God, and give me what is mine."

Honor the mundane reality that supports one part of your life. Give Love to God, and in so doing give to the Master what is His, too. Even a gold coin exists because of God, and in creation all is divine. Those who are blind to that can only see gold. So render appropriately, knowing that you have shared God with those who may neither see nor hear.

101

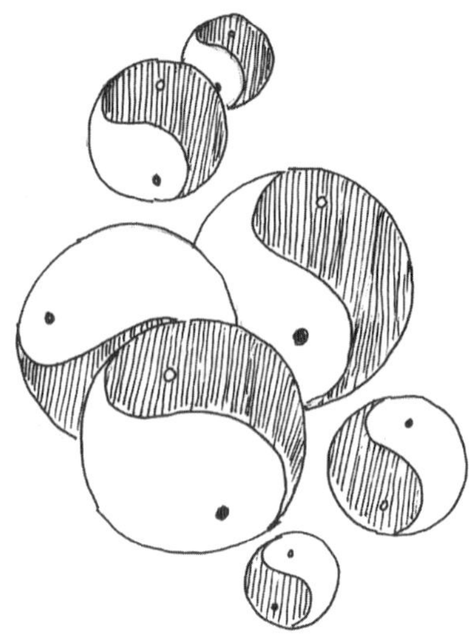

"Whoever does not hate his Father and his mother as I do cannot become my disciple. And whoever does not love his Father and his mother as I do cannot become a disciple to me. For my mother [...] but my true mother gave me life."

Your true Father/Mother who created you will love you unconditionally forever, whereas your earthly parents may only love you conditionally. Yin/yang honors both the father and the mother in the physical body and the Father/Mother who created you before the world was. If your earthly father or mother abused you, forgive them and open your mind and your heart, but don't allow yourself to continue to be abused. God comes first in all things. ("If your eye offends you, pluck it out.")

102

"Woe to the Pharisees, for they are like a dog sleeping in the manger of oxen, for he does not eat nor does he let the oxen eat."

Unfortunate are those who, out of ignorance, control others in what they should learn, or from whom they should learn it, or at what time. Doing these things may keep them from growing, but it also keeps themselves from growing. Dominance, control, dictatorship, and using fear as a wedge, whether in religion, politics, or relationships, is power surrendered. Do not give up your power, for your power is love and free will.

103

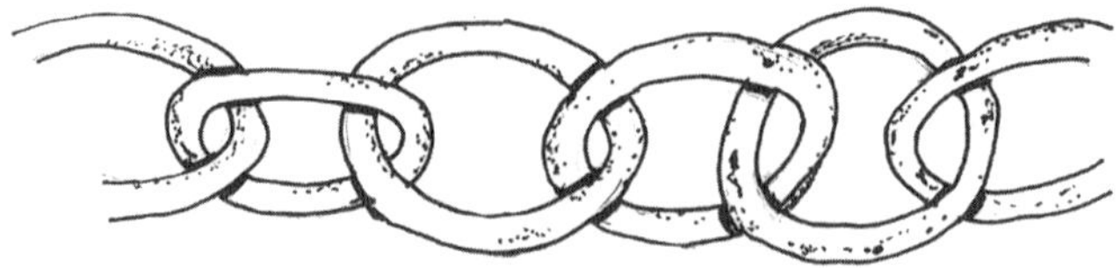

"Fortunate is the man who knows where the brigands will enter, so he may get up, muster his domain, and arm himself before they invade."

Know yourself. Get up and determine your weaknesses and make them your strengths. Use astrology, numerology, dreams, and other gifts of the Spirit to discover the weaknesses and strengths that you chose in this lifetime. Lift the veils.

104

"What is the sin that I have committed,
or where have I been defeated? When the bridegroom leaves
the bridal chamber, then let them fast and pray."

Why bring constrictions into happy moments or opportunities? Celebrate today and forgive yourself and others. When I am with you, be full of days and rejoice. When the occasion is no longer full, then pray and ask for balance. Enter into fasting and prayer joyfully, with an open mind and an open heart. When I am no longer with you, love yourselves and remember me.

105

"He who knows the Father and the Mother will be called the son of a prostitute."

Joshua married a harlot, Rahab from Jericho, and had several daughters. This was an incarnation of God falling in love and having a family. God is your Father/Mother, and so you are the Children of God. The "child of a whore" may refer to previous incarnations, all of which were from the One and expressions of free will choices leading to the present life. One life begets the next, and all are perfect. Judge not, lest ye condemn yourself.

106

"When you make the two one, you will become the sons of man. When you say, 'Mountain, move away,' it will move away."

Obey the Law of One, knowing that the perfect balance of yin/yang is within you physically and spiritually. A "mountain" is the collection of obstacles that are your thought forms from this life and past lives. Where is the blessing in this? When you fully know yourself; and when you fully embrace your whole nature, and when you forgive, release, and let go, then you move these "mountains" out of your path. Then be grateful for them, for they lead you to this very place on your path, and it is your perfection.

107

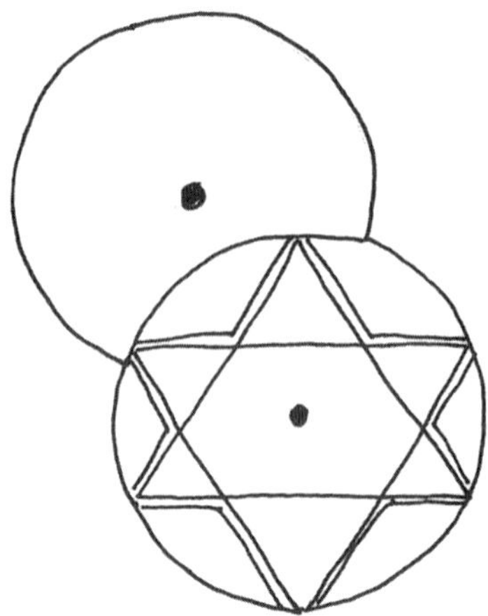

"The Kingdom is like a shepherd who had a hundred sheep. The largest of them went astray. He left the ninety-nine and looked for that one until he found it. When he had gone to such trouble, he said to the sheep, 'I care for you more than the ninety-nine.'"

Using your free will, a part of you may stray and take you into deep travail. Seek that part, find it, and bring it home, for it is your teacher, and all parts of you are worthy of being unconditionally loved. Usually, the greatest obstacles provide the greatest potential for spiritual growth. God is loving you unconditionally in the present moment—so why are you holding out?

108

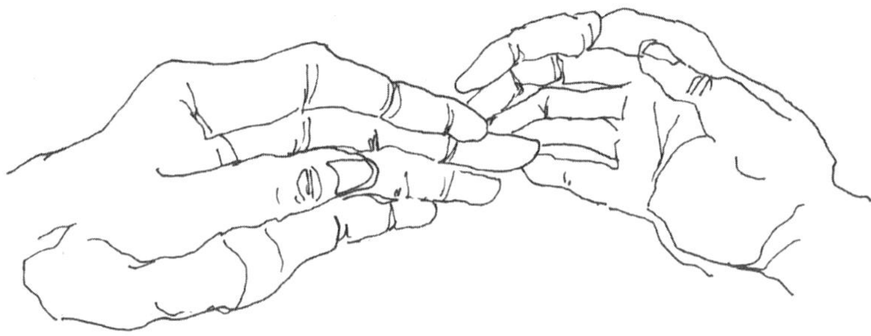

"He who will drink from my mouth will become like me, and I myself shall become he, and the things that are hidden will be revealed to him."

God and I are One. You and God are One. All that you are proceeded from the mouth of God: you were brought into being and given free will. You are gods and goddesses in training to co-create realities. Know that nothing is hidden, except that you believe that you are a separate one from the Source. Come Home and embrace the Whole.

109

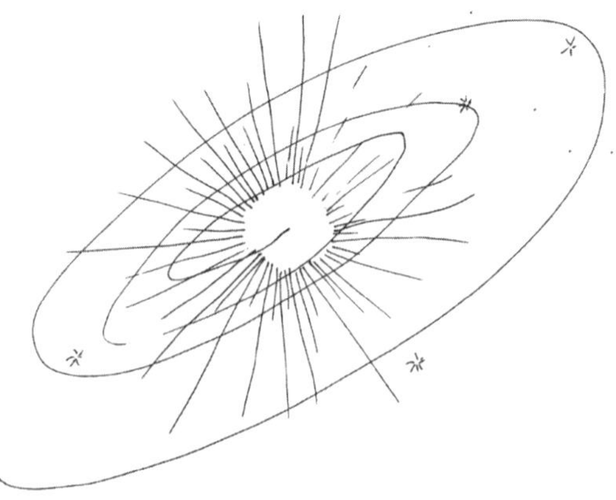

"The Kingdom is like a man who had a hidden treasure in his field without knowing it. When he died he left it to his son. The son did not know about the treasure, and he inherited the field and sold it. The one who bought it went plowing and found the treasure. He began to lend money at interest to whomever he wished."

The spark of God, the divine, is in all things. It is embedded within your heart. But you do not know it so do not perceive it as Truth. You may not have found Truth, and so did not pass it on to your children or those whom you love. Yet another may come to know Truth, realize it in his or her life, and offer it to your neighbor. If something has a price on it, people think that it is worthy, and sometimes when it is freely given people consider it of little or no value or consequence. Give and receive freely. The interest equals what others may ask to give back to you. God's abundance is accomplished.

110

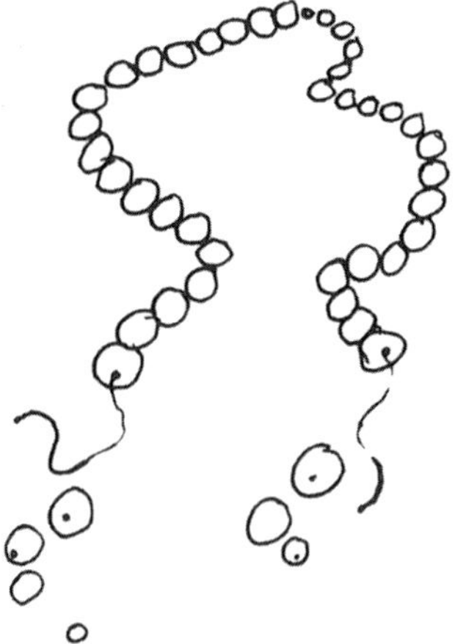

"Whosoever finds the world and becomes rich, let him forsake the world."

Let go of your mundane understanding of physical reality, but know the world and appreciate it, for it, too, is made of the Love of God. Then appreciating it, let go of it. God is the greater good in what He has wrought, and God is all the wealth that there is, and karma brings or takes wealth away from you. So see God in all things, from the greatest to the smallest, for all materialism is of God. Keep the "pearl" for yourself.

111

"The Heavens and the earth will be rolled up in your presence. But the one who lives from the living One will not see death."

The Big Bang took billions of years to unfold, and the Big Crunch takes millions of years for all of creation to return to that single point of origin. Then it begins again. There is no death, and energy is eternal, so you (your soul) are older than the created universe. From age to age, we are all One, eternal and everlasting in Love. The world is a classroom for the soul. Does the student not leave the school when the lessons are accomplished? Graduate and become the master and creator that you are meant to be. Go out into the universe and spread the good news: GOD IS.

112

"Woe to the flesh that depends on the soul,
and woe to the soul that depends on the flesh."

Maintain a balance of knowing freely both the soul and the flesh, for both are interwoven and correspond with one another. When you agreed to come to Earth, you agreed to abide as Spirit in a body. If you only know one or the other, then you only have half of the Truth. Both the soul and the body are God's creation. First the soul and then the physical body.

113

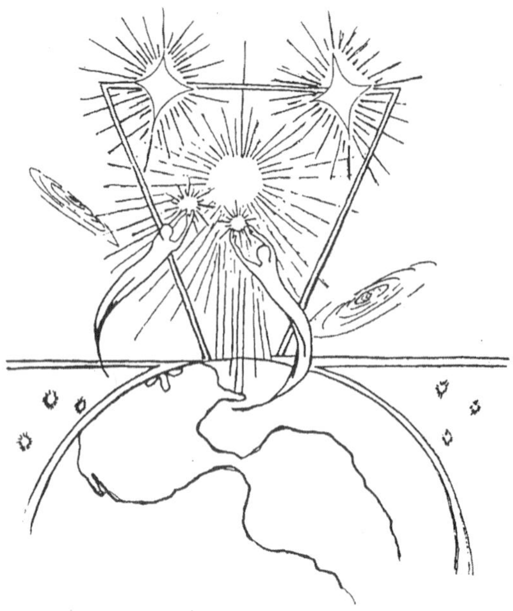

"It [the Kingdom] will not come by waiting for it, and it will not be a matter of saying 'here it is' or 'there it is.' For the Kingdom of the Father is spread out upon the earth, and men do not see it."

The Kingdom, Father/Mother, and Love are all now, and always have been. It is not that it *will* come; it *is* come. At this time, most do not see it nor recognize it, for they are ignorant of the Truth. So go out and teach and heal with their consent, that they might have eyes to see and ears to hear and rejoice.

114

Simon Peter said: "Let Mary leave us, for women are not worthy of life." Jesus said: "I myself shall lead her in order to make her male, so that she too may become a living Spirit resembling you males. Know that every woman who will make herself male will enter the Kingdom of Heaven."

The Master, fully enlightened, having access to total Knowledge, Love, and Compassion, also had a magnificent sense of humor, and here He exhibited it. Understanding all things coupled with humor is marvelous. Education to Oneness has nothing to do with one gender being greater than the other, for yin/yang is all a part of the same Source in Oneness. The Master's mother was his female side incarnate; his yin. He knew this and that she needed nothing—she was perfect just as she was, just as we all are. The men in that age, and to some degree in this one, consider women less than. But this is not God's Truth. There is only God and there is only Good.

So turn this scene around and recognize the humor in it:

Mary said: "Look, here comes Peter and the others, and males are not worthy of life."

The Master replies: "I will guide them to be women. For every man who becomes a woman will inherit the Kingdom of Heaven."

In God's intrusion into the world as Melchizedek, that being was both yin *and* yang—a totally androgynous being. He was not in a physical body, but in a fourth-dimensional body, yet down to earth enough to be able to communicate with physical beings as an avatar. Following Melchizedek's departure from the earth plane through spontaneous combustion (by remembering what is was to be one with the Source), the ensuing efforts to reach out to the human condition were through reincarnation into the physical, first as a woman, and then she would push out her male side, and the two were one. First came Mary, then came Jesus: *one* avatar, yin *and* yang.

Lo, I AM with you always, all of you, even unto the end of the ages and beyond.

Epilogue

The alleged 114 sayings of the Master Jesus continue to be shrouded in scholarly debate. In whatever manner they came into being, these teachings provide a deep and profound soul connection to the God within and to all of life.

Truth Universal is true in every part of Creation, which is God's body. In a fourth-dimensional meditative experience one will encounter Universal Truths. I believe that the mysteries revealed in these 114 sayings are such Truths.

Go into the spark of the divine, which resides in the heart of all humanity. Venture into that sacred space, that Holy of Holies, and thereby see through the veils of the illusions, and find peace.

Whosoever finds these inspirational interpretations
will be filled and have a life more abundant.

Further Readings

The following readings may assist you in your Spiritual journey.

- **Chesbro, Daniel and James Erickson**. *The Order of Melchizedek: Love, Willing Service, and Fulfillment.* Forres, Scotland: Findhorn Press, 2010.
- **Farr, Sidney Saylor**. *Tom Sawyer and the Spiritual Whirlwind.* Berea, KY: Omchamois Publishing, LLC, 2000.
- **Farr, Sidney Saylor**. *What Tom Sawyer Learned from Dying.* Norfolk, VA: Hampton Roads Publishing Company, Inc., 1993.
- **Read, Anne. Edgar Cayce** on Jesus and His Church. New York, NY: Grand Central Publishing, 1983.
- **Regardie, Israel and Marc Allen (Ed)**. *The Art of True Healing.* Novato, CA: New World Library, 1997.
- **Sanderfur, Glenn**. *Lives of the Master: The Rest of Jesus' Story.* Virginia Beach, VA: The Edgar Cayce Foundation, 1988.
- **Smedes, Lewis B**. *Forgive and Forget: Healing the Hurts We Don't Deserve.* New York, NY: Simon & Schuster Pocket Books, 1984.

ALSO BY **REV. DANIEL CHESBRO**
WITH **REV. JAMES ERICKSON**

The Order of Melchizedek

LOVE, WILLING SERVICE, & FULLFILMENT

The teachings of Melchizedek—a totally balanced, authoritative incarnation of Christ prior to that of Jesus—on topics such as reincarnation, spiritual development, and free will, are presented in this manual that relates a positive approach to the current transitional stage of spiritual evolution.

Contending that the unconditional love of God is bombarding the earth in an influx of neutrinos, this account provides a history of Melchizedek, who is a major influence in both the New and Old Testaments but is vastly understudied in most churches. Promoting a harmonious view of religion—where there is one God, understood and worshiped in a variety of different ways, each serving a purpose to those worshipping and to the overall understanding of spirituality—this testament to the Order is both down-to-earth and profound.

ISBN 978-1-84409-502-5

FINDHORN PRESS

Life-Changing Books

For a complete catalogue,
please contact:

Findhorn Press Ltd
117-121 High Street,
Forres IV36 1AB,
Scotland, UK

t +44 (0)1309 690582
f +44 (0)131 777 2711
e info@findhornpress.com

or consult our catalogue online
(with secure order facility) on
www.findhornpress.com

For information on the Findhorn Foundation:
www.findhorn.org

Findhorn Press is committed to preserving ancient forests and natural resources. We elected to print this title on 30% post consumer recycled paper, processed chlorine free. As a result, for this printing, we have saved:

4 Trees (40' tall and 6-8" diameter)
2 Million BTUs of Total Energy
357 Pounds of Greenhouse Gases
1,935 Gallons of Wastewater
130 Pounds of Solid Waste

Findhorn Press made this paper choice because our printer, Thomson-Shore, Inc., is a member of Green Press Initiative, a nonprofit program dedicated to supporting authors, publishers, and suppliers in their efforts to reduce their use of fiber obtained from endangered forests.

For more information, visit www.greenpressinitiative.org

Environmental impact estimates were made using the Environmental Defense Paper Calculator. For more information visit: www.papercalculator.org.

MIX
Paper from responsible sources
FSC® C013483